GERALDINE PELLES is a consultant to the Institute for the Social Study of the Arts in New York City. A former staff member of the Museum of Modern Art, she has also been a political analyst for the United States Department of State and a lecturer in art history and in sociology at Brooklyn College. Dr. Pelles holds degrees from the University of Wisconsin and Columbia University and has studied at the Sorbonne in Paris as a Fulbright scholar. Her article "The Image of the Artist," which appeared in the *Journal of Aesthetics and Art Criticism* and which in an enlarged form comprises a section of this book, occasioned high praise from sociologists, psychologists, and art historians alike.

GERALDINE PELLES

ART, ARTISTS & SOCIETY

Origins *of* a Modern Dilemma

Painting in England and France

1750-1850

PRENTICE-HALL, INC. Englewood Cliffs, N.J.

A SPECTRUM BOOK

© 1963 by

PRENTICE-HALL, INC.

Englewood Cliffs, N.J.

All rights reserved. No part of this book may
be reproduced in any form, by mimeograph
or any other means, without permission in
writing from the publishers.

*Library of Congress
Catalog Card No.: 63-18803*

PRINTED IN THE UNITED STATES OF AMERICA—C

Preface

This study would not have been undertaken but for the suggestion of Professor Meyer Schapiro of Columbia University that I make a comparative, developmental study of painting in England and France during the late eighteenth and early nineteenth century, in terms of my interest in social psychology. I am also very grateful to Professor Ernst H. Gombrich, Director of the Warburg Institute, University of London, for his stimulating criticism and many constructive suggestions. I wish to thank Dr. Leo Deuel for his helpful comments, and Mr. James A. Guiher, Jr., Mrs. Priscilla Hiss, and Mr. Walter Langsam for their editorial contributions to the publication of this book.

Some of the material in this book originally appeared in an article, "The Image of the Artist," by the author in the *Journal of Aesthetics and Art Criticism* (Winter, 1962). Grateful acknowledgment is also made for permission to use excerpts from the following books: *The Journal of Eugène Delacroix,* translated by Walter Pach (Copyright, 1937, by Covici, Friede, Inc. Copyright, 1948, by Crown Publishers. Reprinted by permission of Crown Publishers, Inc.); Charles Baudelaire, *The Mirror of Art,* translated and edited by Jonathan Mayne (Phaidon Press, Ltd., 1955); and C. R. Leslie, *Memoirs of the Life of John Constable* (Phaidon Press, Ltd., 1951).

G.P.

Table *of* Contents

List *of* Illustrations

Introduction

After surviving more than half a century of attacks as nonart or anti-art, various styles of modern painting continue to flourish despite their ambiguity of form and content. Yet, aside from conferring social prestige and serving as a commodity for investment, or as a decorative appendage to homes or public buildings, painting seems to have little place in our technological twentieth century except as a font of psychological discontents and fulfillments.

Living art or, more exactly, living artists who receive the payments or commissions that make the creation of art possible, cannot depend on the kind of support that formerly sustained them. For painting no longer has the same uses it had for thousands of years as an integral part of the institutions of a culture, such as clan, state or church, but is largely dependent upon institutions of its own—the galleries and museums of the small world of the art world. Despite signs that the public's interest in art is growing—mushrooming attendance at lectures, museums and exhibitions, large sales of art books, the entry of Sears Roebuck into the business of selling original paintings to a mass market —publicly or privately supported museums and a few wealthy connoisseurs remain its mainstay.

Paradoxically, as its ties with the community have become more restricted, art has come to be considered more closely related to the entire quality of the life of a culture and of human beings, a symbol of the finest values the culture has to offer. So potent is the very idea of art that even detractors of modern painting usually assume that "real" art is a good in the same vague but certain way that religion is a good— though they may not look at pictures any more frequently than they attend church. Art seems a counteragent to the machine and technology which, despite teachings like those of the Bauhaus, are still widely felt to be antagonistic to human values. In our mass society, possession or appreciation of art is also a sign of belonging to an elite of intellect or feeling. Modern art, in particular, has come to be cherished as an emblem of freedom and spontaneity, as a liberating agent for basic impulses which are repressed individually and restrained socially, and even as an instrument with the power to raise the spiritual tone of the community.

Thus the painter, monetarily insecure, is often idealized (when not scorned as a Bohemian or some other type of nonconformist) as a free, sincere, rebellious spirit whose personality and creative activity may elicit more attention than the work of art itself. And since many of the descriptive terms of art refer not merely to its formal aspects but to mental and emotional qualities that characterize social and personal life, such as rationality and irrationality, intensity, impulsiveness and sensitivity, the terms are often applied to the artist's life as well as to his work. So despite the precariousness and often the painfulness of their interrelationship, art, artists, and society are bound together in a sort of infernal triangle.

The symbolically elevated and institutionally displaced position of art leaves in a dilemma the painter and the members of the public who care about art. The artist often has to choose between creating works the public may not like or understand and creating more widely acceptable or comprehensible works that may violate his own aesthetic values. The public often has to choose between specifying standards that may be stultifying to the artist and accepting almost any work out of fear of harming an entity considered to be a social and personal good.

Laymen, as well as the experts who try to guide the perplexed through the maze of modern painting, tend to think about art in terms of individual or social experience: as self-expression (in which the artist projects his feelings or unconscious onto the canvas), as the expression or reflection of an environment, and as communication (which, in stressing the reaction of the audience as well as the action of the artist, also relies on the idea of art as expression). At one extreme, art becomes a kind of auto-psychotherapy; at the other, a weapon in the cold war, as a symbol of liberty or authoritarianism, inventiveness, or decadence.

Since the concepts of art as expression enter into both the creation and the acceptance of works of art, it is important in facing the dilemma

of painters and publics to clarify the ways in which art may or may not
reveal or indeed affect a person or a milieu.

It has long been recognized that certain styles of art—which, like
styles of life, are patterned ways of doing something—seem to be characteristic of certain societies. In the second half of the eighteenth century, Johann Winckelmann, that influential popularizer of archaeological
discoveries, believed he could divine the "noble simplicity and quiet
grandeur" of the Greek soul from classical statues.[1] In our day, some
writers claim to be able to read the state of the world from its art.[2]

On the other hand, there is a tendency among writers in various fields
—psychology and the social sciences as well as the arts—to visualize art
not as a simple mirror of the world, but as a sort of X ray or telescope
revealing what is invisible in common experience and even (notably in
the writings of Jung) defying the limitations of time and space to make
the most remote epochs accessible to us through a universal language
of visual symbolism, or (in the work of Gestalt psychologists[3]) to
examine what may be certain universal constants of form. These theories
do not, however, account for the phenomenon of change in styles (in
form and in treatment of themes that may indeed be widespread) which
is characteristic of the art of advanced civilizations and a distinguishing
feature of our rapidly changing and varied modern art.

The most direct way to consider the nature of change in styles and
the notion of art as expression is to trace and analyze the development
of art in relation to its milieu over a period of time. Then we should
take account of the complexity both of art and its environment, and the
subtlety of their interrelationships. If art expresses or reflects its world,
we have to decide what in the world it is expressing. But here we have
a difficulty. The expressiveness of visual art is deceptively direct. Unlike
music and literature which unfold in time, it makes its impact at a
glance, though its meanings may be as elusive as those of a sonnet or
a sonata. Not only is this true of abstract styles: the Surrealists used
an ultrarealistic technique deliberately to create an art of high ambiguity.
And if twentieth-century art reveals its world, what aspects of this
constantly changing world does it express? Violence and restlessness, one
thinks before many a Picasso or a Pollock. But what of the tenderness
in another Picasso, the elegance and ease in a Matisse, or the patient
calculation in a Mondrian?

In a pluralistic society such as ours, it is especially difficult to relate art styles to social entities, events, forces, or attitudes in which we ourselves feel enmeshed in a unique kind of cultural crisis. Moreover, the rapid pace of change drives the situation out of focus. For our experience of the present is somewhat like a kaleidoscope whose dazzling patterns are subject to change at any moment; we are not always aware when changes take place or what it is that changes until a certain amount of time has passed for the transformation to become clear.

We can make the problem, if not more simple, at least more manageable, by viewing a situation in the past which we can see more sharply and with greater detachment than our own times. In order to understand contemporary art's precarious ground against its genetic background, we should also choose a period to which we are intimately attached.

But in the continuum of history, where is the end and where is the beginning? The obvious choice of locale is France, the cradle and until recently the center of modern art. The time, according to some of the greatest Impressionist and Expressionist painters whose work made possible subsequent abstract styles, the early nineteenth century. To Manet, Whistler, Renoir, and Van Gogh, the father of modern art was the French Romantic, Delacroix, who lived from 1798 to 1863. But to Delacroix and Géricault, who are regarded as the originators of Romantic painting in France, the father of their art was David, a favorite under Louis XVI and later official painter of the French Revolution and of Napoleon. David's Neoclassicism was acknowledged to be the antithesis of the Rococo which was the characteristic style of the first half of the eighteenth century.

To twentieth-century eyes, many of the major works of the late eighteenth and early nineteenth century look rather old-fashioned in form, technique, and themes. Nevertheless, the main aspects of contemporary musings, theories, and problems concerning the art of painting emerged at that time. Although many of the ideas and practices in art and facets of the social situation of art and artist had been present in previous epochs, a dramatic quickening of pace occurred which signalized a new era in artistic as well as in social, economic, and political life. Strands which had appeared previously coalesced to form a new pattern which came forth vividly and which in substance prevails today. Particularly in the 1820s and 1830s, the apparently negative factors of alienation and ambiguity became for many persons positive attractions.

Even the arsenal of panegyrics and vituperations was similar to our own. Change itself became a virtue together with independence, originality, boldness, and spontaneity among the criteria which, through the years, have constituted a canon by which works and whole styles of art are created.

The general phenomenon of cultural change has, of course, been studied extensively. Many scholars believe in common that immanent forces or processes are responsible for changes in art and in society. Within this basic assumption, their theories contrast sharply. According to various writers, the developmental force resides in an inner logic of the forms themselves or in the art tradition; or in a world soul, the soul of an age or spirit of the times.[4] The genesis of our day has often been traced to that vague complex known as "Romanticism." Thus the critic Sir Herbert Read refers to "the social and intellectual forces that from the beginning of the Romantic movement had been transforming the civilization of the Western world. The visual arts, and all the arts, are in this respect deeply involved, both as cause and symptom, in the general process of history."[5]

From a sociological point of view, the most provocative writings to stem from a belief in immanent development in history are those based on the theory of historical materialism, since they purport to be the most attentive to social realities.[6] According to this theory, as it has been applied to the period we are going to discuss, works of art are reactions to social conditions and art styles are vehicles of the ideology of certain classes in society. It is assumed that certain emotional and ideological characteristics are attached to certain social classes at particular times; and the style corresponding to a social class is said to partake of the emotional and ideological characteristics that are supposed to be intrinsic to that class. Thus such terms as "bourgeois sentimentality" and "aristocratic frivolity" are used in describing aspects of a class or an art style. The terminology and conceptual framework of politics are also used in speaking about art because of the intimate connection art is said to have with the class struggle in the economic and political changes and revolutions: "The prevailing power relationships are expressed in the world of art."[7] Changes in styles are said to correspond to changes in the social situation occurring in terms of the class struggle: we read of an "historically inevitable style" which "accurately reflected its social background."[8]

In our study, however, artists, who create works of art, rather than forces which may exert pressures upon them, will be the basis for discussion. Yet even such an approach is beset with difficulties of its own. For artists as well as art are the stuff of which theories and myths are made.

In recent years, there has been a tendency to dissolve specific traits, skills, or values of artists and art in the generalized attributes of a grand creative process. "Creativity is not, in my judgment, restricted to some particular context," writes the psychologist Carl Rogers. "Our definition makes no distinction regarding the degree of creativity, since this too is a value judgment extremely variable in nature. The action of the child inventing a new game with his playmates; Einstein formulating a theory of relativity; the housewife devising a new sauce for the meat; a young author writing his first novel." [9]

Many psychologists and psychiatrists, as well as laymen, critics, and artists themselves, continue to speak of "the artist" as if he is a special type of person. Some, continuing an earlier stress on psychopathology, regard him as a kind of mental or emotional invalid for whom art is an attempted self-cure. Others, following such founding fathers of modern psychology as Janet and Jung, regard him with awe and virtually as a superman. However, since the 1930s, no differentiation of the artist as a distinct personality type has been found in evidence offered by psychological tests, which show that artists are not temperamentally unlike other persons and that they differ among themselves more than they differ from unselected groups of people. So poorly defined is the hypothetical figure of the artist that judges in one series of experiments were unable to make good predictions, from Rorschach protocols, as to whether or not the subject was an artist; because of the nebulous social image of the artist, the judges had to fall back on private frames of reference.[10]

A number of psychoanalysts of different orientations, notably Rank, Kris, and Schilder, have written of the artist as a person whose tendencies unfold in a specific context. Even Freud, though he believed artists may have a strong constitutional predisposition to neurosis, wrote that art is "a path from phantasy back again to reality," through which the artist "opens out to others the way back to the comfort and consolation of their own unconscious sources of pleasure, and so reaps their gratitude and admiration; then he has won—through his phantasy—

what before he could only win in phantasy: honour, power, and the love of women." [11]

How romantic! Yet this is not surprising. For the greatest of psychiatrists created his own image of the artist in the historical frame of reference to which all of us, still, are heirs.

Although there is no theory adequate to explain art or artists, we can use certain safeguards to restrain personal idiosyncrasy as we select data from the bewildering amount of material that clouds contemporary and historical perspectives. To avoid generalizing from the greatest artists, we shall also include a number of minor figures; when possible we shall let them speak for themselves, from their letters and journals.

Similarly, to avoid generalizing from the art of one country, we shall compare developments in France with those in England where, in fact, painting was in some respects more advanced. And to avoid attributing to the whole development what may be characteristic of only one aspect of the art, we shall look at the paintings from various points of view, choosing key aspects of the subject matter and form, and concentrating on the material, intellectual, and emotional factors in the artistic and social situations that seem most relevant to the nature of the painters' choices in creating the forms and imagery of the art which developed into our own.

In the absence of a general theory to explain all of human behavior, of which painting is one of the crowning achievements, the admission of so many variables will necessarily leave many problems unsolved. Questions will emerge as part of a grand debate that may have no end. For though our comparative approach will help empirically to clarify the record, neither history nor even our contemporary scene is a laboratory in which data can be safely restricted by experimental design without sacrificing the rich complexity of human affairs for a misleading simplicity. Hypotheses and interpretations should allow for, even if they cannot fully explain, the intricacy of human acts and the shifting of manifest and latent factors observed by psychoanalysts in individuals and recognized by anthropologists and sociologists in social life. The following chapters are intended not as a definitive map but as an exploration of the largely uncharted territory of the social psychology of art.

TWO

Rebels & Revolutions

A youth trying to choose a career in early nineteenth-century England or France found himself caught up in the most rapid and drastic changes that had yet occurred in the Western world. If he aspired to a vocation and not merely an occupation, his choice was particularly difficult.

For it was harder than ever to form intense attachments and loyalties under the new conditions set in motion by the economic, social, ideological, and political revolutions of the previous century—conditions which altered the structure and texture of society and the way men conducted their lives and envisaged the world and themselves. Although people were aware that profound changes had taken place which made their times very different from previous ages and that, in fact, they lived in a new age, it was not easy to fathom all dimensions of the transformation. Writers who grew up during those years tried to schematize the tensions and explosions of the century as opposing camps within society: Carlyle pictured the dandies and the drudges, Disraeli the "two nations" of rich and poor, Balzac the avaricious and the generous, Musset the enthusiastic and the quiescent, Tocqueville the conformist and the free.

In the early 1800s, a young man might hope to find at least enthusiasm through the battles of the Napoleonic wars and, if a Frenchman, to feel that he was directly engaged in creating a new world where libertarian ideals, spread by the Enlightenment and proclaimed by the great Revolution of 1789, might prevail. But the years after the wars brought fear and disillusionment to both countries. The English dreaded civil unrest among the new class of factory hands created by a mushrooming industry and the farmers dispossessed by land enclosures. In a defeated France, the Restoration of the Bourbons in 1814 afforded few meaningful channels of action for the first generation since the Revolution without a glorious cause to champion. Their elders mourned the younger generation as composed of "uncertain, skeptical, despairing young men." [1]

If a youth decided to pursue art, he found that it afforded greater freedom of choice than ever before in imagery and forms, including the freedom to change his choice. Some observers feared that change itself had become a norm in the multiplicity and variability of styles. One evening in 1825 at the salon of Baron Gérard, who had been one of Napoleon's favorite painters, the critic Delécluze, a former pupil of David, worried about "this fickleness of tastes, in habits and customs, which makes everything pass before our eyes with the speed of light, not leaving the spirit or the heart time to become attached to anything." [2]

The events of those years provided dramatic themes for artists to paint and distribute widely to the public through color prints. In the opening years of the century, Englishmen painted battlefields strewn with dead Frenchmen, while Frenchmen exhibited Napoleon Boneparte on a white horse leading his troops to victory. In the following decades, there were scenes to paint from the wars of Greece in the 1820s and then the July Revolution of 1830 which overthrew the Bourbons and installed as King of the French Louis Philippe, whose bourgeois manners led him to be called the Citizen King.

Artists also found subject matter in the Industrial Revolution, particularly in England where it developed earlier than in France. In pictures depicting such subjects as blast furnaces and iron forges which Joseph Wright of Derby painted from about 1766 to 1775, a whole range of subjects that had previously been confined almost entirely to popular art and technical illustration entered the orbit of the fine arts.

The new technology also extended the geographical horizons of art. The beginnings of steamboat, express coach, and then railroad transportation opened up whole new worlds of time, space, and tempo,[3] encouraging artists to turn their steps and eyes in new directions. Whereas Rome had been the mecca of painters for centuries, Turner had no central destination for his wanderings over the continent as well as his own country. Rome continued to be a mecca for Flaxman as it had been for David, for the Empire painters who went there in the wake of Napoleon's armies, for Ingres and other winners of the Prix de Rome, and even for younger painters like Corot. And Rome, ancient or modern, is present in their art. But two of the greatest painters, Delacroix and Constable, never made the pilgrimage. Delacroix visited, instead, Eng-

The Louvre, Paris. Archives photographiques

Delacroix, *Portrait of Chopin,* 1838

land where he had friends, and Morocco and Algeria; Wilkie and Decamps traveled to the Levant as well as through Europe. The shift in locale from the ancient classical world shows in their paintings of North African spectacles, hunts, and harems. Constable, however, preferred to stay near the fields, woods, and streams of his native land.

Among the favorite themes were sentimental or satirical renditions of the life and mores of the times, the history of past ages, portraits, and seascapes. Landscapes were coming into greater prominence. And along with the continuing popularity of conversation and genre pieces, there was a revival of interest in the early Italian, Flemish, and Dutch masters, and in the Rococo.

But a deep change had occurred in the dominant mood of art during the course of a century. In the early nineteenth century, there are few echoes of French Rococo *fêtes galantes* or untroubled English conversation pieces, few smiling faces or convivial groups, much pain and loneliness, and little joy untouched by suffering. From the Rococo play with life as a game, art had become serious drama, often pervaded by a taste for the macabre and strange which entered into music and literature as well as painting. Earlier in the eighteenth century, a sweet sadness had sometimes been attached to reverie, as in Watteau's painting of festive ladies and courtiers on a pilgrimage to the mythical Isle of Cythera. It is a century of time and feeling away from the searing melancholy of Delacroix's portrait of Chopin (1838) and from the terror in his painting (1822) of Dante and Vergil traversing Hell in a small boat, and in the countless pictures of flimsy barques tossing on raging seas.

Scores of canvases show solitary figures, isolated from easy human contacts, or enveloped in their thoughts. Delacroix painted George Sand in 1838 with severely heavy coiffure and shadows that weigh down her profile, serving to cast her glance inward. Even groups of people are often shut off from the outside world and partially obscured from one another. The eighteenth-century interior into which light streams from outdoors or scintillates with the brilliance of innumerable candles is transformed into such a picture as Gérard's painting of his salon, a dark room lighted falteringly by a single lamp.

The most basic choice a young painter would have to make involved not subject matter, but form, and particularly the Romantic or Neoclassical styles.

Neoclassical art, as epitomized by such works as *The Oath of the Horatii* and *The Death of Socrates* which David painted in the 1780s, restrains figures in a monochromatic world centered within the picture frame, where clearly delineated shapes are traced in simple planes of action. Although the general norms of this style were continued by David's pupils, who were the outstanding painters under the Empire, they used brighter colors and, as in the works of Gros and Girodet, more excited movements and even fantasy. Girodet and Ingres developed a more undulating, sensuous manner, anticipated and inspired by the drawings of the English sculptor and designer for Wedgwood, John Flaxman. This art survived far into the nineteenth century in the work of Ingres and his many pupils.

A young painter in the 1820s would most likely try to paint in the newer Romantic vein—according to some writers, as a revolt against Neoclassicism. Through wavy outlines, diagonals, many accents of color, and dispersed lights and shadows, Romantic art combined the competing centers of the Rococo with the drama of the Baroque. And like the Baroque, it once again enveloped the spectator.

Although an embryonic or proto-Romantic art had existed in France before the Revolution in the works of David's contemporaries, the Romantic style matured some twenty-five years earlier in England where Turner and Constable were active in the opening years of the nineteenth century. In France the storm clouds—flamelike hair and smouldering glances, more daring brushwork and crowded or precariously stabilized compositions—appeared already on canvases under the Directory and the Empire. But the Romantic style in French painting did not materialize until after Waterloo.

Many artists were among the thousands of tourists who crossed the Channel in both directions after the period of revolution and warfare that had lasted twenty-five years. Visiting Paris in the wake of the occupying British armies, Benjamin Haydon, classicistic painter of lofty subjects, and David Wilkie, the most popular genre painter of his time, admired the skillful rendering of detail in works that Gérard, Gros, and other artists of the defeated Empire had painted for Napoleon.

A great admirer of much English art was the outstanding member of the newer generation of French painters, Théodore Géricault, who had begun to exhibit in the Salons of the Empire. Disappointed by the unfavorable reception of his picture of a shipwrecked group, *The Raft of the Medusa,* in 1819, he went to Britain where people were willing to pay admission to see the huge canvas (today generally considered to be the first monumental Romantic painting in France) when it toured the country. Like his friend Eugène Delacroix who visited London six years later, he was fascinated by the sights of the city, the splendid horses, the color and vivacity of touch in English painting. He was particularly impressed by the use of pigment in the landscapes of John Constable which he praised to his fellow artists in France. At the same time, he continued to revere David, paying a visit of homage to him in exile in Belgium where he had withdrawn upon the Restoration of the Bourbons.

After Géricault's death at thirty-three as the result of a fall from a horse (ironically, some of his most dashing pictures are of horses), Delacroix came to be recognized as the leading painter of the new trend from among the many gifted artists who were exploring the new possibilities. Although they did not emulate David's severity of style and theme, they studied the works of other pre-Revolutionary painters, and admired Neoclassicists like Gros and Ingres, as well as the early Italians and masters of the High Renaissance, Baroque, and Rococo. Some of them were tremendously impressed by Constable's art, which they became acquainted with first through a small painting that made the rounds of the studios and then through the exhibition in Paris of several of his works, including *The Hay Wain*.[4] But two of the other English artists we most admire, Turner and Blake, were little known in France at this time.

After its exciting appearance, Romantic painting thrived for only a brief period in both countries. In the 1830s, French critics spoke of a countermovement whose parentage and direction they attributed to Ingres. It was said to be bringing art back from "eccentric tendencies" to "solidity, truth," and toward "healthy ideas of good taste and reason." As early as 1832, even such a prominent Romantic writer as Lamartine was proclaiming the superiority of the antique, generally thought to be the province of the Neoclassicists, over medieval subject matter which, though associated with the Romantics, Neoclassicists (including Ingres) had painted for a long time. Many Romantic painters, including Delacroix, used classical themes, as indeed they had done in their student days. Many of them veered toward a more classicist style as well— Sigalon (who was discouraged after the failure of his *Athalia*) as early as 1826; and in 1831 Louis Boulanger, the protégé of Victor Hugo; and Champmartin, who had been called the equal of Delacroix. Eugène Devéria and Ary Scheffer, who in the 1820s had been outstanding contenders for recognition as leaders of the new trend, also changed their styles. After 1834 Romantic works appeared in diminishing numbers in the Salons.[5] Hugo was unable to find another band of young painters to serve as a claque for *Les Burgraves* in 1843 as they had for *Hernani* thirteen years earlier. After the 1830s, Delacroix was the only really important figure in Romantic painting in France, as Berlioz was in music.

The decline was even more drastic in England, for it affected all of art and not only Romanticism. In 1822 Constable prophesied, "The art will go out; there will be no genuine painting in England in thirty years." [6] After Flaxman's death in 1826, Neoclassical art was virtually nonexistent in England. Haydon failed in his attempt to introduce a lofty, classicistic style and, heavily in debt, committed suicide in 1846. There were some shifts in a more elevated or a more tempestuous direction, such as the deeply felt personal drive of David Wilkie, who changed his popular anecdotal painting at the high point of his career for a more exalted art, and a fashion for stormy subjects in the pictures of John Martin. However, except for some eccentric exhibition pieces and works by the aging Turner, whose paintings grew increasingly bold, English art in general declined in vigor after the 1930s. Developments which were to culminate in Impressionism were snuffed out in England where they had been most advanced, but continued to grow amidst the fluctuations of taste and practice in France.

During its heyday, Romanticism in France was often attacked as formless and even as diseased—charges which also had been leveled against romantic tendencies by Goethe, though perhaps in a moment of irritation. Although Romanticism in French painting had been in process of formation for many years, the sensation caused by the exhibition of Delacroix's *Massacre of Chios* in 1824, the year of Géricault's death, brought it vividly into awareness as a new and controversial style. Gros, who had helped the impecunious young man buy a frame for his painting of Dante and Vergil in Hell two years previously, branded his new work as "the massacre of painting." The *Journal de Commerce* observed, "Romanticism is not just ridiculous; it is a disease, like somnambulism or epilepsy. A romantic is a man whose spirit begins to change; one should pity him, speak reason to him, lead him back little by little; but one cannot make him the subject of a play; he is rather the subject for a medical thesis." [7]

In England Romanticism as such never became an issue, even though the paintings of Constable and Turner were often subjected to withering criticism. Much of the opposition in France was chauvinistic, for many Frenchmen tended to regard Romanticism as English and Neoclassicism as French, both in origin and spirit. At a time they were fighting a large part of Europe, Frenchmen considered classicism as the national, as opposed to a foreign, element, associating it with the Golden Age of Louis XIV, to which they looked back for emblems of glory. Napoleon ordered destroyed as a menace to French culture the first edition (1810) of *De l'Allemagne* in which Mme. de Staël introduced writers to the complex of feelings and ideas embraced by German literary romanticism. With the fall of Napoleon, even medieval epics, which had fascinated the Emperor, temporarily lost favor because they were identified with the English victor.

During the Restoration, Romanticism was attacked as infected with foreign religious as well as political tendencies. The ultramontanes Bonald and Lamennais believed Romantic mysticism "came forth from Protestantism, from which it gets its fundamental principle of independence, and that essential lack of unity, and that vagueness which characterizes it." [8]

But aside from epithet, what was Romanticism? Already in 1824, the uses of the term were so diverse and contradictory that a group of eminent authorities embarked on a project of discovering what Romanticism was by collecting definitions and characterizations of it—a project that ended in disillusionment after "twelve years of suffering."

The confusion persists today, compounded by the passage of time. The twentieth-century philosopher, Arthur O. Lovejoy, surveying the literature, found that the word "romantic" has come to mean so many things, that by itself it means nothing.[9] "Romanticism" has been used in an almost unrestrained fashion to embrace long spans of time and virtually all aspects of culture and society. A label for profoundly different ideas, it does not even seem to have a common denominator. The first great Romantic has variously been designated as the Serpent in the Garden of Eden, Plato, Francis Bacon, Rousseau, and Kant. Romanticism's offspring are the French Revolution, the Oxford Movement, the Return to Rome, the Return to the State of Nature, the philosophies of Hegel, Schopenhauer and Nietzsche, individualism, anarchy, authoritarianism, existentialism.

Although Romanticism is often used as a diagnostic term for the maladies or blessings of an age, the same point of reference is used for varying reasons. Some say "the classic temper studies the past, the romantic temper neglects it," while others find Romanticism to be "the cult of the extinct." Mme. de Staël located its origins in the Middle Ages; various early twentieth-century writers identified it with the spirit of the French Revolution. Lasserre in *Le Péril mystique* found the chief cause of woe in the Revolution's breach with the past; Sellière in *Le Mal romantique* identified Romanticism with "the spirit of the Revolution in that in which it is rational, Stoic, Cartesian, classical."

Locating its origins in humanism, the critic T. E. Hulme rejected it. However, the psychiatrist Gregory Zilboorg, writing that humanism is but a sixteenth-century name for what later came to be called romanticism, praised the "romantic trend, which put the accent on self-observation, introspection, and understanding of feelings and emotions and their role in human behavior." A talented young man trying to make sense out of a world ravaged by World War II, Alex Comfort, wrote, "Romanticism, the belief in the human conflict against the Universe and against power, seems to me to be the driving force of all art and of all science which deserves the name." Applying the notion of romanticism to personality, the psychoanalyst Otto Rank distinguished between the classical type of artist, which includes the greatest artists, who are free of parallelism between their life and their work, and the romantic type whose creativity has a compensatory character. He contended that the same artist may during the course of his life develop from the romantic to the classical type: "The mature artist can only be born from victory over the romantic in himself." [10]

With their entanglement in a web of political, psychological, and sociological meanings, some of these ideas also enter into aesthetic conceptions of Romanticism. In fact, like the terms for most art styles before the twentieth century, the word "romantic" was not originally applied to visual art. Although long used to refer to something reminiscent of the medieval romances, "romantic" did not designate an art style until the late eighteenth or early nineteenth century. Nor did the word "classical" originate in visual art. "A classic" has been, since the ancient Romans, something or someone canonized by admiration. The term "classical" evokes visions of restraint, harmony, and stability, and "neo-classicism" suggests a revival of something already old. In contrast, Romanticism may seem revolutionary and the Romantic, a rebel—not only in art but in politics as well.

Indeed, some French artists participated actively in the military and political events of the times. Théodore Géricault served briefly as a member of the guard of Louis XVIII, though more for love of the brilliant uniforms and splendid horses than out of political motivation. The attacks Daumier made on Louis Philippe's regime in his cartoons earned him imprisonment for six months. Ary Scheffer (a Dutchman who, like so many other artists from all over Europe, made his home in Paris, the new art capital), was a member of the conspiratorial Carbonari under the Restoration, and he and Paul Huet mounted the barricades in 1830 and again in 1848, when a revolution overthrew the bourgeois monarchy, preparing the way for the Second Empire of Louis Napoleon.

Other prominent artists, like Eugène Delacroix and Camille Corot, never took an active part in politics, and during his long, prolific career, Delacroix painted only one monumental canvas of a contemporary event on his native soil, *Liberty Leading the People* in the July Revolution. Nevertheless, in his *Journal,* one of the most extensive records ever kept by a great painter, he displays a profound interest in the social and political world. After 1830, as the ineptitude of the monarchy of the Citizen King dashed the high hopes of its initial supporters, Delacroix became skeptical of all political machinations and even chided his friend George Sand for her humanitarian sympathies.

In England, where the absence of a political revolution provided fewer occasions for militant engagement in social strife, the post-Revolutionary shock of the generation of Wordsworth and Burke lingered on, intensifying fears of internal chaos and delaying badly needed social reforms. William Blake, who had marched through the streets wearing the symbolic red cap and was openly critical of the state of society, was one of many who were arrested on suspicion of sedition. The atmosphere fostered conservative attitudes. As subjects for murals for Parliament, Haydon, the classicizing painter and friend of Keats and Wordsworth, proposed in 1812, "First to show the horrors of anarchy; then the injustice of democracy; then the cruelty of despotism; the infamies of revolution; then the beauty of justice; and to conclude with limited monarchy and its blessings." [11] The most advanced painter of the times, John Constable, objected even to the rather mild Reform Bill of 1830, explaining, "What makes me dread this tremendous attack on the constitution of the country is, that the wisest and best of the Lords are seriously and firmly objecting to it; and it goes to give the government into the hands of the rabble and dregs of the people, and the devil's agents on earth, the agitators." [12]

Many artists, whether or not they participated directly in the social and political eruptions, regarded art itself as an avenue of revolution, personal or social. Still fired by the ideals of the Enlightenment and the great Revolution, they hoped to find means of emotional and intellectual restoration through the arts as an area of timeless and timely verities.

Youths did not visualize themselves as painters, composers, or writers merely in terms of the work they did standing before an easel or meditating at a desk. Their very association with this type of work seemed to be a declaration of independence against the ordinary life of the times and an affirmation of the mythical free individual who had become an ideal in the intellectual and political developments of the past hundred years. For a feminist like George Sand, this sort of attraction was particularly strong. She recalled in her autobiography, "To be an artist! Yes, I wanted to be one, not only to escape from the material jail where property, large or small, imprisons us in a circle of odious little preoccupations, but to isolate myself from the control of opinion . . . to live away from the prejudices of the world." [13]

Young men did not find art compelling merely as a means of asserting personal independence. Being an artist could make one feel significant

The Louvre, Paris. Archives photographiques

Delacroix, *Liberty Leading the People*, 1830

by belonging to a community of the illustrious—for example, the projected Council of Newton in which the Comte de Saint-Simon called for painters to sit beside scientists, writers, and composers.

In practicing art, they had a sense also of contributing to the world, and even of healing or changing it, not only through the didactic effects of subject matter, as formerly, but through the activity of art itself. "With works of Art their Armies meet . . . ," chanted Blake.

Along with the Utopian socialist Proudhon, some artists believed that art was the moral expression of societies and ought to be their guide. In tune with Utopian and socialist thought, Franz Liszt declared, "The regeneration of art is a social regeneration." [14] Many artists con-

sidered themselves to be the leaders of a cause, no less than a humanitarian, political, or religious leader, or a physician who ministers to the
sick. With the decline of confidence in a super-historical sphere throughout the eighteenth century, a conviction grew that art and artists were
imbued with a quasi-religious as well as a moral and social mission.

In the 1820s and 1830s, art in France acquired the aura of a religious
revival, which the neo-Christian movement itself failed to achieve. Liszt
apostrophized, much as Shelley had done before him, "those of the
elite who seem chosen by God to be witnesses to the great sentiments of
humanity and to be noble depositaries of an ineffable, mysterious, eternal
religion which germinates and grows incessantly in all hearts.[15] Delacroix's friend, the eclectic painter Paul-Joseph Chenavard, planned an
ambitious series of murals for the Pantheon that he hoped would fulfill
the religious and philosophical mission he envisaged for art. Calling his
four assistants his Evangelists, he declared, "I see myself already as the
great priest of a new cult. . . . Art is for me the only means of making
familiar to everyone the philosophic Idea by giving it a body." [16]

The place of the painter in the pantheon of the great was relatively
new. The rise of the painter and painting in the hierarchy of the arts,
and of the arts in the hierarchy of human values, had been slow.[17] Until
the sixteenth century, the three visual arts were not strongly differen-
tiated from the crafts. And until the seventeenth and eighteenth centuries, philosophers had made little distinction between "art" and "fine
art."

The painter, as distinct from the poet, had generally been considered
in antiquity and the Middle Ages as a craftsman, respected for his
manual skill and observation of the outer world. With the revival of
Neoplatonism in the Renaissance, the outstanding painter was held in
awe for his "genius." This endowment had formerly been thought to
be possessed by—or to possess—poets, who, like philosophers and sages,
were believed to have special knowledge of man's intellect and inner experience. Alberti in his treatise *On Painting* (1436) ranked painting
as the highest among the arts, for it "contains a divine force." Thus the
painter, or at least the great painter, seemed a demigod.

As the status of the painter became more exalted in the hierarchy of
human activities, his attributes became less specialized or restricted. His
main activity was considered to reside not just in his hands but primarily
in his brain and spirit. At last the painter was permitted to share in

the role of moral teacher which had been accorded the poet in antiquity and the Middle Ages. He could regard his work not merely as the execution of a commission but as the fulfillment of a calling.

In France "art" attained greater autonomy and status as "fine art" in the seventeenth century, when the founding of the Academy encouraged an extensive theoretical literature on the visual arts which grew steadily throughout the eighteenth century. Art, along with science, was thus elevated to a new place in the hierarchy of intellectual values. Just as there was confusion between science and technology, so also was there confusion about the nature of art: until 1765 the arts still had an intermediate position between *sciences* and *métiers*. The word "art" did not include painting (nor sculpture, nor architecture) until the middle of the eighteenth century.

So gradual was the psychological and social emancipation of artist from craftsman that the words "artist" and "artisan" continued to be used as in the past. In 1719 an important writer on aesthetics, the Abbé Dubos, referred to Michelangelo as an "artisan." As late as 1785, people still spoke of "artists" to whom one gave the task of watching cows. The greater separation of artist from craftsman coincided with the beginnings of the acceleration in the mid-eighteenth century of the displacement of artisans by machines. It also coincided with the dissemination throughout Europe of ideas of the Enlightenment—that intellectual revolution whose influence was to be as profound as the economic and political ones—of the freedom of the individual to determine his own destiny and create his own life, and by implication, his own art. Possibly the first formulation of the idea of art-for-art's-sake occurred around this time,[18] many years before the doctrine of *l'art pour l'art* was promulgated in the 1830s. By 1789 the word "artist" was used more extensively in France. Around 1820 "artistic" became current, and by the mid-1830s there was a vogue for the word "artist" which had become synonymous with "creator."

So it was that, at about the same time it had at last become established, the new system of the fine arts began to disintegrate, leaving the painter in a paradoxical situation in which to view himself and his art. Along with the greater distinction accorded painting and the painter in a relatively autonomous realm, art also came to be regarded as a generalized creative activity, and the artist as the embodiment of a diffuse creative quality. Balzac defined art as a résumé, a synthesis of diverse activities which have the creative faculty in common. "The name artist," wrote Félix Pyat, "does not belong only to poets, painters, sculptors, musicians, architects, actors, dancers; it belongs to all those whose genius has been creative. Is not Dr. Broussais who invented his admirable physiology a great artist?"

While the two views of the painter as craftsman or divine genius continued to exist side by side, the artist seemed increasingly a being who is not removed from the rest of mankind by virtue of strange (wonderful or wicked) constitution. Wordsworth argued in his Preface to *Lyrical Ballads* that the artist is not an esoteric or an overspecialized person, but a man who appeals to the normal interests of mankind. The view was current also among nonartists. Like the universal man of the Renaissance, wrote Lord Wellington, "a painter should be a historian, a philosopher, a politician, as well as a poet and a man of taste." [19]

With the popularization by the French Revolution of the newer ideas of the nonexclusiveness of individual worth, the feeling also grew that *all* men *can* be artists. Blake's disciple, John Linnell, said that his master "claimed the possession of some powers, only in a greater degree than all men possessed, and which they undervalued in themselves, and lost through love of sordid pursuits, pride, vanity, and the unrighteousness of Mammon." [20]

As the new dual image of the artist as a superior being and as an ordinary man became more sharply etched, a feeling of estrangement developed which we can discern in a series of self-portraits and portraits of artists. David and Ingres painted themselves at work before the easel. But the Romantics developed a class of paintings of artists immobilized in the midst of their art. Bonington painted his own melancholy features shrouded in shadows. Géricault portrayed Delacroix at the age of twenty as enclosed in his thoughts or dreams. And he showed an artist alone among the shadows, skulls, and brushes of the studio, propping his head on his hand, as does Michelangelo in a late painting by Delacroix.

Although artists had also felt a sense of loneliness and isolation in the past, now these feelings became a dominant theme. As the self-image of the artist changed against the background of the intellectual, economic, and political revolutions, his new autonomy subjected him to unprecedented pressures and conflicts, both psychological and material.

THREE

*A*rt as an Institution

Despite the inspiration of their mission and the spiritual rewards of associating themselves with high ideals, artists had to face the stringencies of economic reality. Under the new social and institutional arrangements, art became a displaced element of culture many years before the idea of art-for-art's-sake was well developed.

In the Renaissance the idea of *l'art pour l'art* had been implicit in the production of easel paintings, created for an elite group of connoisseurs rather than for a large public. These paintings often had no religious or didactic content or purpose, and the patrons enjoyed them for their own delight. Under the accelerated changes of the eighteenth and early nineteenth century, painters almost completely lost their old function of serving the vital needs of social institutions by making decorations for palaces or altarpieces for churches.

Nevertheless, art did not lose its attractions as a profession. Indeed, the numbers of painters in the early nineteenth century kept pace with and may even have exceeded the rate of the population explosion which had been set off by improvements in sanitary and medical conditions and by the Industrial Revolution. The rate of increase of painters exhibiting in the Salons of France almost doubled over the previous period and continued to mount also during the monarchy of Louis Philippe.[1] Artists continued to find sustenance in the apparently unfavorable environment created by the new hegemony of the middle classes.

The new markets for art were as uncertain as its uses. By the first half of the eighteenth century, French painters were already in dire straits. Through the increasing secularization of life, a sharp decline in church patronage began at that time. In the Salon of 1789, before the outbreak of the Revolution, few religious works appeared; most were mythologies or subjects based on antiquity or French national history.[2] The church continued to commission works after the secular interregnum of the Revolution, so that in response to opportunity and demand, nonreligious artists like Delacroix painted religious themes far into the century. But the survival of religious painting did not result in a revival. In the official Salon of 1831, only twenty-nine of the 3,000 entries dealt with religion.[3] And attempts to concentrate on religious subjects by the so-called School of Lyons, influenced by Ingres' style, resulted in a rather slick art of low vitality.[4]

Royal patronage, a stand-by for French artists, had also declined. In the late seventeenth and early eighteenth century, because of the bankruptcy of Louis XIV's court, there was less demand for ambitious paintings for the walls of palaces. Artists catered to the nobles or rich merchants who wanted pictures smaller in sentiment as well as size for their town houses.

Largely under the impetus of a moralizing current of ideas from England around 1725, the government stepped in to try to salvage the grand style of art, which it also associated with the national glory through the art and academies of the Grand Siècle. It began to put this program into effect in the late 1740s, the time when changes that were to create a new economic and social system had set in on a large scale,[5] and when theoretical writing codified the modern system of the fine arts in almost its final form, separating the mechanical, useful arts from the fine arts (music, poetry, painting, sculpture, and the dance).[6] There was an official attempt to reinstate a loftier tone in art and to emphasize the status of the painter as a moral teacher, which, though vouchsafed him in the Renaissance, had been temporarily submerged by the Rococo style of pleasure as an end in itself. After 1760 the sober trend was accelerated by the new archaeological publications and engravings of paintings inspired by the excavations at Herculaneum and Pompeii. Stimulated by the commissions of successive ministers of Louis XV and Louis XVI, artists were imbued still further with a sense of their duties as *peintres de l'âme*.

Such exalted personages could not be permitted to live in misery. Therefore the program to evoke a more exalted type of art was accompanied by assurances of pensions and of living quarters and studios in the Louvre, and the awarding of various prizes and stipends. The government tried to encourage art in general by establishing art schools in the provinces and by holding exhibitions. Even the opening of the

The Louvre, Paris. Archives photographiques

David, *The Oath of the Horatii,* 1784

Louvre to the public during the Revolution was not a new idea; the

Along with its liberality in admitting more artists to the Academy, the Revolution exercised a selective effect on the variety of themes and styles that flourished under Louis XVI. Four years before the political revolution, a severe and exalted tone had become so pervasive that *Le* establishment of a museum for the purpose of elevating public taste was seriously considered as early as 1747. The Revolution finally gave institutional expression to the idea of the fine arts, and thus implicit recognition to the autonomy of art, when it merged several of the older academies dating from the seventeenth century into the Académie des Beaux Arts.[7]

Journal général de la France spoke of "une révolution frappante" under the direction of Vien. The previous year the leadership of what was also hailed as a "renaissance" had been assumed by Vien's pupil David, whom the government commissioned to paint *The Oath of the Horatii*. This work, with its exploitation of the antique in a restrained style, was hailed as "the most beautiful painting of the century." Even before the *Horatii,* the general revival of seventeenth-century trends had also culminated in a more activated style, with subject matter depicting scenes from the national past, such as Vincent's *President Molé Seized During the Fronde* (1779), which are suggestive of Romantic works to be painted half a century later.[8]

Although David had been the rage among the aristocracy for many years, his sober art might not have found such great extension in France if the Revolution had not adopted it as its official style. In fact, David's severe style flourished for only about ten years, declining with the death of the Revolution. During the Directory and the Empire, it was modified and transformed by the master's pupils and by David himself. If the Revolution had not occurred and made Neoclassicism its official style, French Romanticism might have developed directly out of the revival of neo-Baroque painting. In this light, Romanticism even appears to be a reversion to pre-Revolutionary trends as much as a revolt against Neoclassicism.

The post-Revolutionary governments continued to support art schools and exhibitions, and offered special scholarships and prizes. More and more, museums and exhibitions became the destination for works of art, which acquired the new function of serving these institutions whose purpose in society was the perpetuation of Art. Museums and galleries became the temples and chapels of the substitute religion of art, which virtually became an institution unto itself. They also came to have an effect on art styles, as the older forms of patronage continued to do, and were a sustenance for painting and painters at moments of crisis.

Despite an apparently less favorable environment for painting in England, where government encouragement of the arts was late and sporadic, Neoclassicism as well as Romanticism matured earlier in the works of English painters. In fact, French painters before the Revolution eagerly studied engravings of paintings by Gavin Hamilton, works which were fifteen to twenty years more advanced in style than the

Palais Bourbon, Paris. Courtesy Assemblée Nationale

Vincent, *President Molé Seized During the Fronde,* 1779

canvases of Vien. Except for the work of imported foreign artists, native English painting had been virtually dormant from the Middle Ages until the eighteenth century, when it revived in the art of Hogarth. At the same time, beginning with the formation of the Dilettanti Society in 1734 by a group of gentlemen who had acquired a taste for art during their travels in Italy, a number of private groups were established for the encouragement of the arts. Many gentlefolk, men as well as women, engaged in painting as well as in collecting as a pastime. But aside from

George III's private commissions to his favorite, the American Benjamin West, there was little state encouragement until the founding of the Royal Academy in 1769 through the efforts of that lover of High Art, the master portraitist Sir Joshua Reynolds.[9] By that time, the French Academy had been fostering art in France for one hundred and twenty-one years. In England, however, except for the Royal Academy's prizes and exhibitions, official government patronage remained desultory.

The sudden flowering of English painting in the late eighteenth century may have been connected with the greater prestige conferred upon it by the founding of the Royal Academy. And in the first third of the nineteenth century, under the leadership of the Prince Regent who became George IV, many among the aristocrats and the wealthy were patrons of contemporary painting, especially the work of West, Lawrence, and Turner. William IV, who ascended the throne in 1830, had an attitude toward art quite different from that of the fashionable circle of the Regency, and of his French counterpart Louis Philippe, who was a collector himself and friendly with artists. When shown a favorite painting of George IV, he observed, "It seems pretty—I daresay it is, my brother was very fond of this sort of nicknackery. Damned expensive taste though. Take it away, take it away." [10]

It was also more difficult for English painters to get adequate training or even to see masterpieces from which they might learn. Before 1818, when Henry Sass founded a drawing class at Bloomsbury, there was no place in London where artists could be trained for entrance to the Royal Academy schools. Many students, including the ambitious young David Wilkie, down from the Scottish highlands to make his way in the world, had to practice anatomy by drawing themselves in the nude.[11]

Poor artists and students without the proper connections found their only picture galleries in the auction rooms. In the first two decades of the century, before the opening of the National Gallery in 1824, most of the private collections were still closed to the public. In 1819 a French visitor complained that English servants extorted money for entrance to supposedly public exhibitions, adding, "The pleasures of the fine arts are enjoyed here only by the well-to-do. Why are the common people excluded from them? In Paris the poorest Frenchman may visit our magnificent Louvre." [12]

With all their hardships, many English artists felt there was a basic incompatibility between the state and the artist. Although some painters, like Haydon who lobbied for commissions for architectural decorations, courted official support for the arts, others were wary of official entanglements. When the government proposed to provide a new site and building for the Royal Academy, some Academicians objected on the ground that such aid would involve state control.[13] Uneasiness about government support was not new. Hogarth had opposed attempts in the late 1740s to found a Royal Academy on the French model on the ground that its art education could only serve to create a large number of bad painters, thus causing the price of pictures to drop still further, and leaving a handful of teachers at the Academy to glory in their titles.[14]

This was not mere crankiness nor a rationalization of the situation prevailing in England. For even in France governmental channels for the support of art aroused opposition. Voltaire and the Encyclopedists claimed that academies foster pedestrian talent rather than genius; it is interesting that Fragonard and Greuze never became members of the Academy. As governmental support grew stronger, it became more absolutist. In the 1770s the king's minister of public works, the Comte d'Angiveller, issued restraining orders against some exhibitions that painters tried to hold independently of the Academy in protest against its exclusivist policies, which the new ideas of the freedom of the individual made increasingly intolerable.[15] David may, in fact, have supported the Revolution as much from disgust with the official art organization as from political idealism.[16]

Opposition to the governmental art authority in France continued in the early nineteenth century, so that gradually, advanced art developed almost entirely outside the orbit of officialdom. The irritations evoked by official taste led many painters, Neoclassicists and Romantics alike, to refuse to exhibit at the Salon after the 1830s. Ingres joined their numbers after 1837, Delacroix after 1859.

Thus despite official patronage in France, French painters, like those in England, needed and wanted other outlets for their work. As they had throughout the eighteenth century, they continued to find a market among private individuals, who now more than ever became an important source of patronage and sales. During the Restoration and the

July monarchy, the flourishing of many rich private galleries testified to the existence of a lively demand for all styles. The very structure of the extra-academic art world emphasized the separation of painters from the mainstream of society. Reaching many of his purchasers through that middleman, the art dealer, and, with the growth of journalism, through the critics (those mediators or would-be pontiffs whose influence on public opinion remains unclear to this day), the painter had less direct contact with connoisseurs than formerly. He found little steady support from the fluctuating tastes and fortunes and the speculative buying of a public which, though enlarged, did not compare in size with the public for the new industrial and scientific exhibitions in England and France. The vagaries of the art market in both countries seem familiar to us. For instance, when Morland was mistakenly believed to have died in 1797 (he actually died in 1804), his works rose in value by 200 per cent.[17]

The problem of making a living exerted strong pressures even upon French painters of established reputation. Few were able to wait until the age of fifty-one, like Corot who was subsidized by his prosperous shopkeeper parents, before selling a painting. Even in the sixteenth and seventeenth centuries, when the effects of art's relative autonomy were already being felt, many of the greatest masters did not rely solely on commissioned work for their income. The most fortunate, like Velásquez and Rubens, were highly respected courtiers, or, like Giovanni Bellini, Titian or Dürer, they had salaried public and clerical offices or regular grants. Others might try to sell their works in shops, in the streets, at church doors, and at fairs. Some held a second job: Jan Steen in a brewery, Jacob Ruisdael as a barber-surgeon, Rembrandt and Vermeer as picture dealers.[18]

In the early nineteenth century, some painters resorted to schemes of self-help. The debt-ridden Haydon held a raffle for his large *Xenophon's First Sight of the Sea*.[19] In emulation of the English custom of charging admission to exhibitions, David also held such an exhibition of his *Rape of the Sabine Women*. His paintings, except for portraits, had earned him no money from before the Revolution until the Empire, though his rich wife's income saved him from financial misery.[20] In France in the 1830s, a group of painters tried to deal with their financial problems by forming a sort of artists' cooperative, agreeing that each in turn would work at his art for a year at the expense of the others.[21]

Of course, painters could still fall back on the time-honored tradition of portraiture to make a living. Portrait painting had long had an especially prominent place in England, where the Protestant religion excluded many other types of subjects commonly enjoyed in France. In 1712 *The Spectator* had commented:

No nation in the world delights so much in having their own, or Friends' or Relatives' Pictures; whether from their own National good-nature or having a love to Painting, and not being encouraged in the great article of Religious Pictures, which the Purity of our worship refuses the free use of, or from whatever causes.[22]

Perhaps more than any other type, portrait painting subjected the artist to the specifications or vanity of his customers. The French portraitist Mme. Vigée-Lebrun, visiting London in 1802, was shocked by the extremes of accommodation to the patrons' tastes. "I went to the principal painters," she wrote in her memoirs, "and was mightily astonished to see that they all had a large room full of portraits with nothing but the heads done. I asked them why they thus exhibited their pictures before finishing them. They all answered that the persons who had posed were satisfied with being seen and mentioned, and that besides, the sketch made, half the price was paid in advance, when the painter was satisfied too."[23]

Many painters had a strong aversion to what they felt to be the indignities of such work. Blake refused to paint portraits at all. He left the protection of his patron Hayley who, he wrote to his brother James in 1803, "thinks to turn me into a Portrait Painter as he did poor Romney, but this he nor all the devils in hell will never do. . . . I now defy the worst & fear not while I am true to myself which I will be."[24]

Other artists, bowing to financial expediency, were willing to compromise, executing portraits reluctantly, as a means to the end of making a living. In early nineteenth-century England where there were few commissions other than for portraits, even a great artist like Constable painted the likenesses of country squires, in order to make enough money to marry. In France, Chassériau, the painter of the 1840s who, as a prodigy of eleven, had been a pupil of Ingres and who later fused this early influence with that of the Romantics, reasoned, "I wish to do enough portraits to become well known and to make money, in order to achieve the independence necessary for fulfilling the duties of a painter." [25]

Even some of the finest portraitists and most celebrated artists complained that portraiture conflicted with their aspirations to execute noble, didactic works. Ingres felt he was being mistreated by "enemies" during his earlier years in Italy, not because he was without employment, but because he was paid for painting and drawing portraits rather than what he considered more elevated subjects. Mme. Ingres said that "after every portrait, M. Ingres declared that he would do no more, that he was a history painter and not a draughtsman of bourgeois." [26] James Opie, a contemporary of Blake, succeeded so well in painting portraits that he was known as the English Rembrandt. But he regarded portraiture, which he cultivated out of financial necessity, as "the parasite of personal vanity"; it was the duty of the true painter "to teach, and not to please—if he aspires, like Zeuxis, to paint for eternity." [27]

The most fashionable portraitist, Sir Thomas Lawrence, felt he had prostituted the technical gifts that had attracted attention while he was still a child. Although he boasted of his skill in the difficult task of making "an awkward Figure strait and erect and grand without stiffness," he mentioned also that the moments are rare "that I am satisfied with myself." In his later years, after looking again at *Satan,* which he had painted in the grand manner before embarking on his uninterrupted career as portraitist to high society, he wrote to a friend in 1827, "I am return'd most heavily Depress'd in Spirit from the strong impression of the past dreadful waste of time and improvidence of my Life and Talent." [28]

In artists' distaste for executing portraits, there was something at stake more fundamental than a sense of discovery as a technical explorer or of mission as a moral teacher. More than any other type of subject, the portrait involves the ego of the painter as he literally confronts the ego of the sitter. The necessity of subjecting himself, eye to eye, to the will of the purchaser entails a self-subordination that probably had always annoyed painters, but became a prime irritant with their increased professional and social status. For instance, a great artist in the 1500s might express scorn for his public who, he believed, in contrast with his acquiescence to their desires in the past, should assent to the ideas and practice of the artist. [29] In the early nineteenth century, the element of free choice for artists was accentuated as never before, and became not only a condition but a requisite for the creation of art. Although especially conspicuous in the case of portraiture, this ambivalence between pleasing oneself and pleasing the customer pervaded all types of art. It induced a generalized hostility toward patrons whose very existence implied the patronizing, that terrible threat to one's self-esteem, which wounded painters as artists and as human beings.

In their hostility toward patrons and the idea of patronage, in their conviction that the public should follow them rather than command, artists were suspicious of those very institutions which made painting more widely salable than ever before. The impersonal atmosphere of the museum seemed to many to weaken the impact of art. Delécluze believed museums were *hôpitaux de l'art* "which one enters in spite of himself with the cold and impartial spirit of a critic judging art." David agreed, "In the final analysis, an immense museum of statues and paintings is made to produce critics like Winckelmann rather than real artists." Many believed that the proliferation of galleries, which encouraged painting specifically for the purpose of an exhibition, resulted in mediocrity and superficial exhibitionism.[30]

Artists even attacked the well-meant financial grant. Géricault pointed out that government schools and prizes, however good in intention, did not form men of genius. The French students in Italy, he said, "become accustomed to living off the government's money and pass the best years of their lives in repose and security. They leave having lost their energy and no longer knowing how to try."[31]

Some painters rejected the style or type of art that had gained them favor with their public (or publics) and had brought them money and fame. After several attacks of ill health brought on by mental crises, David Wilkie dropped the manner which had made him the most popular painter of his day. Decamps, regretting that he had ever painted his small pictures of the faubourgs, marketplaces, and landscape about Paris, went to Switzerland and Greece in search of subjects through which he hoped he could realize a superior power he felt within himself. The successful illustrator Achille Devéria, dissatisfied with doing chic things for his numerous clientèle, took a job in the print department of the Bibliothèque Nationale in 1849 in order to make a living in some other way.[32] Gros refused to paint the Battle of Jena at the command of the court of Louis Philippe. "Having already done so many pictures of that type," he declared, referring to his paintings for Napoleon which though banned by the Restoration, could again be exhibited publicly in 1830, "I feel the need of returning to subjects more appropriate to the study of art"—by which he meant classical paintings in the manner of his master David.[33]

Others worked simultaneously in more than one style. The Swiss Fuseli was celebrated for paintings in the grand manner he had learned in the Mengs circle in Italy before settling in England, but he also had admirers for the pornographic and dream pictures by which he is best known today.

Turner successfully worked in two styles and, like Hogarth before him, catered to different kinds of publics. His election to the Academy was in recognition of works painstakingly faithful to the appearances of nature, and he earned a great deal of money through engravings of the landscape and architecture of England. Although his paintings were hung in choice places in the official exhibitions, a far cry from the earliest showings of his work on the door of his father's barbershop, the bold style of many of his landscapes, seascapes, and mythologies was received with mixed enthusiasm. A critic greeted his *Calais Pier* in 1803 as "a lamentable proof of genius losing itself in affectation and absurdity." His *Slave Ship* (1840) was "clap-trap" to the American painter Inness, and the *Steamer in a Snowstorm* (1842) was called soapsuds and whitewash by critics, in the same spirit in which they mocked "Constable's snow." [34] Stung by adverse criticism, Turner complained that he was forced to do "mappy" engravings for the general public in order to make a living. In fact, however, he also had a public of admirers for his advanced works, so that even during the last twenty years of his life, as his style grew bolder, he sold considerably more of his exhibited oils than he retained.[35]

Some artists cultivated only one style, refusing even temporarily to practice a more conventional art which would have brought swifter rewards. Delacroix led a precarious existence for several years after the financial decline of his wealthy family, seldom selling a painting or a lithograph. But he refused to compromise his ideas in exchange for an easy success. When, after the exhibition of his sadistic and coloristic

Death of Sardanapalus in 1827, the director of fine arts told him that he would have to change his style in order to get government commissions, Delacroix refused, although it meant "for five years, no more commissions were received, no more pictures bought. You can imagine what that lack of employment meant for me, when I felt capable of covering a whole city with paintings." [36]

Constable's wait for success was considerably longer and especially trying for a family man with six children to support. Before their marriage, his sweetheart could not understand why "a professional man should shun society. Surely it cannot be the way to promote his interest. Why you should no longer be anxious for fame is what I cannot understand." Later, reflecting on his failure to win financial success with his landscapes, Constable wrote to his friend and occasional patron, the Reverend John Fisher, nephew of the Bishop of Salisbury (who commissioned him to paint the cathedral), "I now fear (for my family's sake) I shall never make a popular artist, a gentleman and ladies' painter. But I am spared making a fool of myself." [37] Rescue finally arrived in 1828, nine years before his death, when he came into his father-in-law's legacy.

Blake was rescued neither by an inheritance nor by the sort of patronage he felt he could accept. A contemporary noted, "His works were looked coldly on by the world, and were only esteemed by men of poetic minds, or those who were fond of things out of the common way. He earned a little fun but no money by these speculations." [38] Except for three uneasy years under the patronage of William Hayley, gentleman of letters, Blake supported himself and his wife—sometimes barely —by the engraver's trade he had learned as a boy. He was once forced to accept charity from that benevolent squirearchy, the Royal Academy, which never accepted him as a member.

While Blake's poverty was all too real, the facts of Ingres' life do not bear out his fulminations about sufferings caused by lack of appreciation. Nevertheless, his complaints often have been taken literally, making him seem the prototype of the long-suffering, misunderstood genius. In stories about the hardships of artists, as of other persons, one must be prepared for exaggerations based on various types and degrees of eccentricity or self-dramatization. Ingres' mental anguish was no doubt real, but it was based on what even adulatory admirers of the time recognized to be neurotic symptoms—feelings of persecution based on deep-seated pangs of insecurity rather than on mistreatment by an unappreciative world.

At the age of twenty, Ingres won the Prix de Rome on which he lived until 1811 when he was thirty-one, making it possible for him to paint works that were not commissioned and remained unsold for many years. During his subsequent stay in Rome, he also painted canvases for Napoleon, and upon returning to Paris in 1824, he was acclaimed by artists, officials, and connoisseurs who assured his success. In 1837 he was named president of the Institut which replaced the old Academy.

But Ingres could not bear even isolated failures, which he faced with flight or refusal to finish a commission. Crushed by adverse criticism of his *St. Symphorien* in 1834, he fled to Italy, refusing commissions for Nôtre-Dame-de-Lorette and the Pantheon, even though he had dreamed of renewing the grand tradition of architectural painting. When another opportunity offered itself through the Duc de Luynes's order for murals illustrating the Golden Age and the Iron Age in the Château de Dampierre, Ingres was plagued by his own uncertainties. Imagining that he was being treated badly, he left the work unfinished after having made studies for it over a period of ten years, from 1840 to 1850. To welcome him home from Rome in 1841, Louis Philippe feted him at Versailles, and he was honored at a huge banquet at which Berlioz conducted a program of Gluck and Weber. But at the pinnacle of fame in the 1850s, Ingres, now a Senator of the Empire of Napoleon III, still saw threatening shadows. "If not forced to stay in Paris, I would be off right away. . . . But where to go? To Italy? Infected also. Ah! imperious necessity that keeps me here where I suffer." [39]

The laments of Ingres have been taken for fact in terms of the myth that suffering is a natural accompaniment for the life of the artist. The image of the agonized artist, who sports as stigmata of a holy war against the Philistines his often self-inflicted wounds, was dear to artists and public alike. Those artists for whom art was a substitute religion could have the satisfaction of visualizing themselves—or at least of dramatizing themselves to the public—as martyrs who, like apostles of other religions, were persecuted for their beliefs. Ignoring contrary evidence in the persons of such artists as Velásquez and Rubens, Liszt wrote, "Moral initiation, the manifestation of humanitarian progress, at the price of the most painful sacrifices and devotions exposed to the persecutions of ridicule and envy, such has always been the lot of true artists." [40]

Like all myths, this one also contains much truth, for painters, writers, and musicians had endured material difficulties at least since the days of François Villon. Many persons of the early nineteenth century, including artists themselves, often looked askance at success and a life of ease as threats to artistic integrity. With sentimental idealization of the virtues of poverty, admirers of the impoverished Blake respected him for scorning gifts. Quite seriously, the writer Gustave Planche considered with the landscape painter Paul Huet the hazards of the quick success which is hastened by vitiating publicity: "Today via the newspapers, one arrives and rises more quickly than before. The artist, if he is not careful, soon reaches a state of feverish overexcitement. To keep his intelligence healthy, he must be vigilant about himself every moment of the day." [41]

In a society where more persons were concerned with material success than ever before, such sentiments served as a rationalization of the relative uselessness of the work in which the artist engaged, and as a sort of exoneration from failure to achieve recognition among those Bohemian artists who continued to live in poverty, unlike Ingres' pupil Hippolyte Flandrin who became harried by too many commissions. They could yet hope to achieve respect among intellectuals for leading a life which, though it might entail material hardship, seemed faithful to nobler ideals than those animating the lives of ordinary men. Henri Murger, himself an ex-Bohemian, later became rich and famous with the publication of *The Bohemians of the Latin Quarter,* in which he wrote of "a charming and a terrible life which has its conquerors and its martyrs, and one which we should not enter save in resigning ourselves to submit to the pitiless law *vae victis.*"

Great numbers of French artists seemed to be engaged, not so much in a painful struggle with the outside world but in what appeared to be a civil war within art, a battle of styles that made the literacy Quarrel of the Ancients and Moderns of the seventeenth century look tame. In the 1830s and 1840s, Romantic partisans, with epithets of *momies!* and *grisâtres!* dramatized their displeasure with the subject

matter drawn largely from classical antiquity and with the closed outlines, limited color range, and smooth finish of Ingres' paintings by
turning up their coat collars as if shivering from the cold when they
passed a Neoclassical work. In the medieval and exotic subjects, the
visible brush strokes, and patches of bright and sometimes broken color,
the Neoclassicist demonstrators found justification for their accusations
of *sauvages! Shakespearéens! flamboyants!* One of the worst was *gothique,* which earlier in the century some critics had used as a term of
disparagement for Ingres' own work.[42]

Although the Neoclassical and the Romantic demonstrators appropriated Ingres and Delacroix, respectively, as their leaders, the "battle"
had been slow to develop. Certainly it would be hard to imagine anyone
less a leader than the timid Ingres. Upon the favorable reception of his
Vow of Louis XIII in 1824, he confessed, "I was so surprised by the
talent, and especially by the very skillful execution of my colleagues,
that, without the encouragement given me by Forbin, without the confidence he seemed to have in me, I would not have dared to face those
comparisons.[43]

At the time, another exhibitor in the same Salon, the young Delacroix,
found Ingres' work "charming." [44] In the early 1830s, Achille Devéria,
Alfred Johannot, and other young Romantics spoke of Ingres as one
of themselves, not only artistically, but in age. Gautier eulogized "the
paintings by our great young masters, Delacroix, Ingres, Decamps." [45]
However, the enthusiasms of contemporaries often blind them to facts.
Actually, while Decamps was thirty and Delacroix was thirty-five,
Ingres was fifty-three, a generation apart from the younger men. He
belonged, instead, to the generation of other fellow-pupils of David, the
Empire painters Gros, Gérard, and Girodet.

Moreover, there was no unity of taste within either "camp" in the
battle of styles, and there was no organized program such as was to be
formulated in the twentieth century by the Surrealists and Futurists.
The classicistic illustrations for Homer and Aeschylus by John Flaxman were admired in France by both Romantic and Neoclassical
painters. Even at the height of the Romantic movement, young artists
regarded them as part of their studio equipment.[46] Furthermore, Romantics did not always admire each other's art. Many thought Decamps too
tame, and Delacroix found the works of Turner, Hugo, and Dumas too
extravagant and the music of Berlioz "a heroic mess." [47]

Nevertheless, fanned by the propagandists, friction between these two artists—the greatest nineteenth-century Neoclassicist and the greatest French Romantic—developed over the years. For Ingres, Delacroix was one of those omnipresent "enemies" by whom he had imagined himself threatened since early manhood. Perhaps stamping his feet in a characteristic gesture, Ingres greeted Delacroix's belated election to the Institut in 1859 crying, "Behold the wolf in the fold!" [48] During the past thirty years, the paintings the young Delacroix had found "charming" had come to be models for the eclectic academic style that pervaded the Second Empire, a style he attacked as a pastiche of "antiques and mongrel Raphaelism which is that of Ingres and those who follow him." At the Exposition of 1855, this association led Delacroix at first to reject Ingres' section: "The dominating thing in it, to a great degree, is the ridiculous; it is the complete expression of an incomplete intelligence." Yet Delacroix was still able to face the art on its own terms, so that two weeks later on a return visit he wrote, "The group of Ingres' things seemed to me better than it did the first time, and I am thankful to him for many fine qualities that he gets." [49]

In England a battle of styles after the French pattern did not develop, for there was no firmly entrenched, official classicistic tradition in painting to oppose an insurgent Romanticism. Nor did large groups of artists and student cohorts exist to fabricate such an issue and fan it into flame. Association among painters was much more limited than in France. A favored few might hope to be invited to evening receptions held by the aristocratic and wealthy subscribers to the British Institution. But practically the only place they met regularly was at the Royal Academy, which was like an exclusive gentlemen's club, or in evenings "at home" like any other good member of the middle class. [50]

In France, however, there were channels for the formation of an *esprit de corps* among artists analogous to that of other professional groups such as doctors, lawyers, and priests. As a continuation and expansion of the salon world of the eighteenth century, it was the custom to meet, lounge, and talk in studios, cafés, salons, and cénacles which clustered about a major figure. Through these groups, even an ordinary painter had access to the best in manners and ideas. In the salon of the painter Baron Gérard he could speak with an eminent scientist like Alexander von Humboldt. Painters and writers met in Charles Nodier's *Salon de l'Arsenal* in the 1820s and in Victor Hugo's cénacle in the 1830s. And Hugo, Sainte-Beuve, and Musset used to frequent the house of the painters Eugène and Achille Devéria: Romanticism was said to be at home at the Devérias.[51]

Artists in France constituted a distinct social group, while in England painters as well as writers[52] regarded their problems as those of a professional group rather than a distinct class. In this way, French artists were separated from, or separated themselves from, their main patrons while overtaking them on the social ladder, at the same time that painting rose in the hierarchy of the arts.

Even in the past a favored few artists had been able to rise in social status by being granted official honors. Some may have been attracted to art as others had been to science in the seventeenth century, as a way of associating with persons of high rank.[53] In continuation of the practice of honoring outstanding artists, which had been established since the Renaissance, painters were honored with knighthoods in England, and in France with titles—Baron for Gros and Gérard, Senator for Ingres, Chevalier de la Légion d'Honneur for Decamps and Chassériau. Daumier, remaining true to his political convictions, refused an honorary award from the Second Empire. But in general, such recognition was highly coveted.

However, it was no longer necessary for a painter to receive titles and honors or to be a great artist in order to rise in social status. In the eighteenth century painters were generally of lower class origin, or they were sons of artists who, by and large, were still tainted by their former association with crafts. By the early nineteenth century, particularly in France where the greater prestige of art stemming from its long tradition helped make it a more socially esteemed profession, painters belonged to the same social stratum as the middle classes that were steadily increasing in power and whose upper echelon became the dominant group in the 1830s. Over a period of three or four generations, French painters tended to be of prosperous bourgeois origin, like David, Géricault, Delacroix (whose natural father may have been Talleyrand), and Chassériau. Or their fathers were painters, as with Gros, Ingres, and Flandrin, whose father had been a business man before turning painter.

The French painters, sons of the middle and upper middle class, did not rise to a higher established social stratum by becoming artists. They constituted, instead, what was virtually a new elite class apart from their middle class origins, with little institutions—cafés and cénacles—of its own in addition to the official academy. As an elite, they were in a position to make a sharp division between themselves and the bourgeoisie, a division they often exaggerated and overdramatized. In his *Confession d'un enfant du siècle,* Alfred de Musset wrote of the formation during the Restoration of "two camps: on one side, the exalted, suffering spirits, all the expansive souls who have need of the infinite. . . . On the other side are the men of flesh, inflexible in the midst of material possessions, and they have no other concern than counting their money."

But the real sources of conflict between artist and public did not lie in fancied or real attributes of the newly dominant middle class.[54] In fact, hostility of artists toward the middle class as such did not exist nearly to the same extent across the Channel, where art faced an even graver crisis. Contrary to the situation in France, painters in England tended to be sons of the lower middle class of tradesmen, like Blake whose father was a hosier, Lawrence whose father was an innkeeper, Turner whose father was a barber, and Constable whose father was a miller. Wilkie's father, though a minister, was very poor. An English painter could enter the orbit of the upper middle class if he were elected an Academician, whereupon he acquired the title of Esquire like a born gentleman.

In 1835 when protestations of disgust with the bourgeois had reached a peak among French artists, Haydon thought the salvation of art might lie in the hearts of the middle class, "the men that honour human nature and these form the bulk of the middle classes. Glorious Old England!"[55] Although Haydon's views were colored by his hopes of obtaining official commissions and delivering lectures, they did reflect the lack of large scale discontent among English painters in terms of the class from which they sprang or which they aspired to enter. In relation to the upper middle class, theirs was a process of association, rather than of disassociation as in France.

Just as the greater approximation in style of life between the aristocracy and the middle class in France before the Revolution had resulted

in an inflammatory psychological situation between them, so did the
rise of French artists in the social hierarchy intensify an ambivalence
toward their public which was now, more than ever, made up of persons
of their own social class. Because in their hostility toward the new
patrons French artists were engaged in internal class conflict, they insisted all the more on their status as an elite group, which placed them
above their origins, whether high or humble. And just as their situation
reinvoked the old myths of the artist as rebel and martyr that stem back
to Prometheus and Icarus, it also created the new myth of the Philistine
bourgeois.

In attacking the insensitivity of the bourgeois, French artists
were largely shadow boxing. For there was no one "middle class taste."
In fact, it becomes meaningless and even fallacious to use the names of
social classes as descriptive terms for types of art. For social classes
themselves are not monolithic in their attitudes, and taste is not a
matter of simple like or dislike. Moreover, the acceptance of art as
"great" is related to purposes and values other than the giving of pleasure. For instance, it is not at all certain that even sophisticated Renaissance patrons always "liked" a work of art they bought or commissioned.
Furthermore, there are levels of attention as well as taste. The experiencing of art is something intense and rare, not a constant like breath-
ings of which we are usually unaware. But in everyday life we scarcely
notice the pictures on our walls, and we are often indifferent in the
midst of great art—Mozart becomes a backdrop for the conversation and
laughter of a social gathering.

In the early nineteenth century, as was probably also the case in the
past, most of the public not professionally engaged in art was habitually
indifferent to it. A relatively small sector of the public kept alive the
subculture of art and, in doing so, became a new elite within and beyond
the middle class. In fact, the stratification of artistic taste, as of the
culture in general, corresponded less than ever before with class lines.

With the accelerating economic and political changes, as mobility
from class to class became more fluid and as classes subdivided within

themselves in interests, goals, and ways of life, it became still more difficult to discern artistic tastes according to groups in society. Despite a greater emphasis on equality, complete leveling had not, of course, occurred. For a society is always hierarchical in some way; when one type of division has been reached or dissolved, others take its place. Class distinctions remained very strong in these societies that were egalitarian only in principle. The legal freedom granted by revolutionary victory in France and by successive reforms in England did not abolish class differences and in fact opened other gulfs between men. In 1789 the French upper middle class which, except for caste status, had already been prominent and powerful before the Revolution, came to be a new kind of aristocracy. After 1830 even the king was bourgeois in his style of life. Mrs. Trollope wrote in 1835 that republicans feared the menace to libertarian principles of a new aristocratic bourgeoisie.[56]

The subculture of art enabled both those who had arrived into this new aristocracy and those still on their way up to transcend conventional class differences. Increasingly, the majority middle-class culture assimilated, often by design, many practices and values of the minority aristocratic culture it was supplanting.

For reasons of enjoyment and the social prestige that art collecting has traditionally conferred, individual wealthy members of the middle class had also been patrons and collectors throughout the eighteenth century. After the Revolution, the French upper middle class, which had often been the economic and intellectual power behind the nobility and whose tastes and habits in art had already been highly cultivated under the old regime, tried to continue many practices of the past. It inherited the responsibility of the arts along with problems of political administration. A critic wrote, "Today when art is changing and tends to descend in the family, it is the public which ought to serve it, in the same way as a Leo X, as the Medicis, and as a Napoleon." [57]

Many bourgeois patrons were truly dedicated to art, had highly sophisticated tastes, and respected and were respected by painters. Delacroix himself recognized this to be true. While critical of many aspects of life that he attributed to the hegemony of the middle classes, he was often more irritated by critics and fellow artists than by patrons. Disgusted by academicism and slights of his own work in the 1850s, he referred in his *Journal* to the "good will of the Maecenases" and the public who are taken in by "schools" and artists without talent.[58]

The multiplicity of tastes in the middle class was also characteristic of official circles. The variety and liberality of official taste were a continuation of practices of the old regime, in which there was no uniform "aristocratic taste." In fact, the eighteenth century aristocracy was highly permeated by middle class influences, not only through the ideas of the *philosophes*, but also through close personal contacts such as Louis XV's relationship with the low-born Mme. de Pompadour. Even the unascetic king, though he was bored by the lofty painting sponsored by his ministers, did not interfere with commissions for that type of art. Chardin was given the post of treasurer of the Academy from 1755 to 1774 even though his beautifully simple art, dealing with segments of the everyday world of the bourgeois household, was not in accord with the idealizing trend.[59]

In the early nineteenth century, reception of official honors was even less an index to popularity or style. With the ever greater bureaucratization (already considerable under the old regime) which accompanied the new social and political changes, official taste was suffused with still more tastes than formerly. Patronage was forthcoming even for artists who were considered to be avant-garde. The government of the Restoration purchased the twenty-six-year-old Delacroix's *Massacre of Chios,* and later the July monarchy bought other works from him and commissioned whole mural cycles.[60] Except for landscapists, never favored by officialdom in France, even the bourgeois monarchy did not refuse recognition to artists considered the most audacious of the time; they are represented equally with more traditional painters in the Luxembourg museum.[61]

A conflict and competition for art authority within the government resulted in the paradox that Delacroix, who received expensive governmental commissions, was not elected to the Institut until seven years before his death. Similarly in England, one Neoclassicist, John Flaxman, was an honored member of the Royal Academy (though not until the age of forty-two), while another, Benjamin Haydon, never was elected to that august body but was obliged to accept its alms. The Romantic, Turner, was elected to the Academy at the age of twenty-seven. But Constable, though he had a devoted following of influential persons who included Sir George Beaumont as well as the Fishers, was not made a member until eight years before his death.

None of these groups of governmental authority or social classes was homogeneous enough to secure the community of feeling or interest that is necessary to create a standard of taste or purpose. In France even more than in England, allegiances in terms of class in general and to art in particular were hard to identify with particular groups in society. Partly because the French middle class had been later in obtaining power than its English counterpart, it had a more varied character as it underwent many subdivisions in the successive violent social changes. Despite a greater approximation in the French and English conditions, a writer of the time observed that the middle class of France in the 1820s and 1830s was not as homogeneous as that of England.[62] It did not have such well defined characteristics, consisting as it did of men who were not yet accustomed or reconciled to their new roles—men who had risen into it and aristocrats who had fallen into it during the revolution, as well as the descendants of merchants who had already comprised it in the eighteenth century. The varied character of the middle class, together with the traditional respect for art in France, provided favorable soil for a continued conflict and multiplicity of tastes.

In England as in France, the middle-class public which had purchased art throughout the eighteenth century became a more important purchasing agent than ever. Whether for love of art for itself or as a High Pursuit or for reasons of social prestige, progressive industrial pioneers like Wedgwood and the Arkwrights were patrons of the arts in the second half of the eighteenth century. With the mounting pace and expansion of the Industrial Revolution, the new manufacturing magnates purchased art as they did landed estates in their pursuit of the status of gentry. Particularly after the deaths of Lord de Tabley and Sir George Beaumont in 1827 and 1829, patronage passed out of the hands of the old noble and landed classes as society leveled upward. The new buyers included Vernon, an ex-jobmaster and army contractor, and Sheepshanks, a clothier from Leeds, who left their collections to the nation. Jacob Bell, druggist, donated Frith's *Derby Day* and many other paintings. Wells of Redleaf, ex-sea captain, was a Landseer collector. Bicknell, oil merchant, and Windus, carriagemaker, were two of Turner's chief patrons.[63]

The greater social mobility in England, which travelers from Poggio to Voltaire had noted in the past and which was now accelerated by the economic revolution, was to contribute to the spread of a morality, descended from Puritanism and associated with evangelical religion, that was to be harmful for the newly emergent native painting.

It would be a mistake to attribute solely to religious factors the delayed flowering of English art. Considerably before the Reformation the visual arts had been in eclipse in England, largely because of its remoteness from the continental centers of artistic incubation and creation. The early Puritans, moreover, were not hostile to emotional expression or to art as such, but only prohibited certain subject matter. Indeed, the revival of English art in the eighteenth century coincided with a tide of emotionalized religion.

Nevertheless, a morality that thrived with the reaction caused in England by the excesses of the French Revolution had deep ramifications for artists. The percolation upward of a militant Methodism, which at first in its inflammatory religious aspects provided an outlet for the miseries of the lower classes, gradually led, in a mollified spirit decried by John Wesley, to the pervasal of all classes by an emotional repressiveness that moved Balzac to refer to the "glacial barriers" of the "British personality." The new morality directly affected culture and manners. It intensified the passion for respectability that had become apparent in the last two decades of the eighteenth century with the rise of the new manufacturing classes.[64] In 1800 Wilberforce established his Society for the Reformation of Manners and an Association for the Better Observance of the Sabbath. Old literature was expurgated: Thomas Bowdler's *Family Shakespeare* appeared in 1818, James Plumptre's *Crusoe* in 1828. The Reverend John Trusler, for whom Blake unsuccessfully tried to do some illustrations, wrote *Hogarth Moralized* and *The Way to be Rich and Respectable*.

It is hard to know to what extent the newly pervasive attitudes may have affected the enjoyment of looking at painting, which necessarily engages the senses. Thackeray deplored the absence from English middle-class homes of pictures, except for an occasional portrait, in contrast with the frequency of prints on French walls. But this may have been largely due, as Pye the engraver claimed in 1835, to the excise duty on glass, which made it about eight times more expensive than in France.[65]

Altogether, the atmosphere was a discouraging one for the creation of art. For it fostered a low opinion of the painter as a fellow who actually engages in and does not merely contemplate the sensual and "useless" occupation of painting, a lazy and immoral fellow who misuses valuable time staring at nude models. It is hard to imagine a French painter saying, like Blake, "I myself remember when I thought my pursuit of Art a kind of criminal dissipation & neglect of the main chance, which I hid my face for not being able to abandon as a Passion which is forbidden by Law & Religion." [66]

Many a young Englishman must have hesitated to undertake a career that his unsophisticated fellow countrymen regarded as immoral and effeminate and unworthy of a real man, who should rather aspire to be an industrious builder of industry. Wilkie's grandfather, a miller, could not understand why a young man who displayed a strong bent for mechanics should decide upon an artistic career. "Ah, my mon Davie," he admonished, "it will be a long time ere daubin wi' a stick will do anything for thee." [67] Thackeray noted that, while in France the mere profession of art gave a man a position above his merits, in England a grocer would not allow his daughter to marry an ordinary painter. Even Haydon, who frequently attacked the Royal Academy, admitted that without it artists would be treated as journeymen.[68]

The flowering of art that was fostered by the founding of the Royal Academy in the latter half of the eighteenth century was not able to survive the combined effects of an emotionally repressive atmosphere and flimsy support by tradition and institutions. But despite the frustrations it made artists suffer, the limiting situation had temporary benefits for art.

It was partly because of a constrictive morality that the sensuously disguised genre of landscape was the main vehicle of English Romantic painting. And the very weakness of state patronage freed artists from an entrenched tradition of figure painting, which was associated with the Academy in France. Landscape painting may also have been fostered by the greater dependence of English artists on wealthy private patrons who, because of their manner of life, were in general more attached to the land than were their French counterparts. In the second half of the eighteenth century, when estates became larger in England as a result of the enclosure laws, the French government was breaking up feudal holdings and distributing them to vast numbers of peasant proprietors. By the end of the century, hardly any of the French nobility or gentry still lived in the country. In England, their quite different relationship to the land may have nurtured a taste for landscape painting, which persisted in the nineteenth century among the newly arrived commercial aristocracy who were actively acquiring landed estates along with such other accoutrements of social status as art collections.

Within their institutional limitations, English landscape painters created the most advanced art of the time, an art through which the painter could assert his individuality by means of subjective observation and touch in greater degree than through the better supported art of France, where the old and new institutions of art restricted the artist in the process of sponsoring him. But in France as well, equivalent ideas of individual assertiveness motivated the new painting and led to unprecedented problems for the painter in reaching a public through his art.

FOUR

The Language *of* the Feelings

If a painter wished to address himself to the vast unsophisticated public, an easy solution seemed to be afforded by the realistic anecdote, a favorite type of art in early nineteenth-century England and France, as represented by the pictures of Wilkie in England and later of Meissonier in France. The small size of these paintings made them suitable for middle-class homes, and all tell legible stories with which an ordinary person could feel some familiarity, either through personal experience of life in home, city or country, or through news stories of adventures on the high seas and battlefields. These episodes were painted as the spectator thought he might really see events with his own eyes.

Realistic anecdotal art combined an emotional or psychological appeal with its illustrational interest in such works as Rippingville's painting of 1819, *The Post Office,* whose subject was "the delivery of Letters and Newspapers at the Post Office and the various impressions on the minds of those who peruse them." [1] Of course, easy communicability is not necessarily a sign of superficiality, as we can see in the works of Hogarth and Chardin, of David who was acquainted with Mengs' doctrine that the beautiful appeals to the majority, and of Goya and Daumier, Constable and Corot. In Courbet, Realism even became epic in its glorification of the familiar.

Often "realistic" paintings united democratic intent and high purpose. The idealistic and learned Ruskin praised Wilkie's art "because it touches passions which all feel and expresses truths which we can recognize." [2] But occasionally the purpose of some realistic art seemed too low. Constable disliked the paintings of the seventeenth-century Dutch and Germans, who were enjoying a revival. Of these he wrote, "With them dignity of subject never excluded meanness, and the wretched material introduced into their historical pictures could have led to nothing, or worse than nothing, impressive." [3]

49

Popular realistic paintings were not always simple in style, for even the more naïve sectors of the public are not necessarily impressed by the simple. Wilkie did not like the early Italians, whom Constable admired for their sense of immediacy and naïveté, preferring instead the more studied Raphael and Michelangelo. He praised his Renaissance demigods in terms of the element of ready communication their works contained, declaring, "These seem alone, whatever their talent was, to have addressed themselves to the common sense of mankind. They have indeed this high quality, that the subject is uppermost, and they have more excellence addressed to the unlearned observer than any work I know of." [4]

A painter could not be sure that a careful study of reality or nature would put him in touch with the "unlearned observer," who might be expected to take pleasure in such pictures as the familiar fields painted by Constable. However, Constable's paintings only became popular posthumously. It would appear that realism or naturalism was not a sure route for the artist to the understanding of the public. While this problem was accentuated in the new situation of art and artist, it had not risen suddenly.

Art had always had, aside from its illustrative, didactic, or magical uses, an aesthetic function not open to literary explication. Even when painting had become more "realistic" through the perfection of perspective and chiaroscuro, in the fifteenth and sixteenth centuries artists also satisfied a special demand for obscure allegories among a coterie of learned connoisseurs. They addressed their work specifically to the learned man who, regarding the appreciation of the arts as one of the accomplishments of a *Cortegiano* as delineated in the book (1528) by Count Baldassare Castiglione, prided himself on being able to decipher obscure meanings and special conceits in painting as well as in poetry. The very notion of the fine arts may have crystallized from the conversations in cultured circles in London in the early eighteenth century,[5] when shifts in the economic and social strata increased their size and range of composition. This amateur interest in the arts, while apparently providing a larger enlightened public for the artist and freeing him from the demands of "vulgar" taste, only tantalized him with freedom. For in fact the sophisticated beholder, who thought he knew his own mind and trusted his own judgment, subjected the artist to a close relationship which tended to bring artist and connoisseur together more from the point of view of the spectator than from that of the painter.

The point of view in painting, of artist or of beholder, was not considered to be primarily a matter of visual sensation but of the mind. Thus the Renaissance concern with visual sensation in art was countered by an idealizing tendency which generalized and interpreted the multiple facts given to the eye. At the same time, works of art were thought to be involved with solutions of problems through which, as in science, they added to the body of knowledge. But as contrasted with the sciences, which rest upon the accumulation of knowledge, and a conception of art stemming from antiquity and the Middle Ages as something that can be taught, the revival of Platonism set up another view of the artist as having a divine gift or a divine madness with which he is endowed and which cannot be taught. Despite their differences, these views stress the primacy of individual talent in the arts, recognized as one of their main characteristics in the Académie des Sciences and the Royal Society in the second half of the seventeenth century.[6]

The importance accorded the individual became visible in art early in the Renaissance with the intensification and individualization of facial expressions and gestures. Then in the caricatures of Leonardo da Vinci and Bernini, in Rembrandt's portraits, and in Baroque showpieces for court or church, the imprints of character and the passions on countenance and body were explored and exploited to a far greater degree. With the shift of emphasis from specific details of content to mood or expressiveness, the French Academy issued a handbook which an artist could consult for rendering various expressions.[7]

Analyzing psychologically what Renaissance artists had known in practice, eighteenth-century philosophers also recognized that the images of art were not merely reflections of the world on the retina. Berkeley and Hume sought to eliminate the dualism of "sensation" and "reflection," previously formulated by Locke, by combining them in the term "perception," thus implicitly placing greater stress on the actions and reactions of the individual. Kant went further, replacing Locke's and Hume's idea of the mind as a *tabula rasa* or as "passive wax" molded by sense-experience, with his concept of the mind as an active agent selecting and reconstructing experience. He asserted that we know not by reasoning, but by vivid and immediate feelings.

The new orientation is glimpsed in painting in the generation preceding his own which Kant regarded as the time of the "liberation of man from his self-imposed minority" by the Enlightenment. Sparkling Rococo art lifts the world into the idiosyncratic psychological realm, especially in the art of Watteau which takes courtly ladies and gallants into the make-believe world of an aristocracy that was crumbling in reality. Around the same time, there was an increase in subjects that appealed directly to the feelings and dealt with the life of the middle and lower classes. Such themes had been highly developed in the seventeenth century in Italian and Spanish low-life paintings and in Dutch genre. In the first half of the eighteenth century, with the growing numbers of middle-class buyers and, in France, of aristocrats bored with courtly life, the varieties of the realistic anecdote increased.

Even though their works contrasted with the sentimental conversation piece and the frivolous Rococo, which were the characteristic prevailing arts in their respective countries, Chardin and Hogarth were popular among various social groups. The moralisms of English conversation pieces and the tales of Richardson, along with English philosophy and science, penetrated France, where they reached maudlin heights in the second half of the century in the works of Greuze. Even so intellectual an observer as Diderot extolled them for teaching virtue which was "natural" to man, in contrast with licentious and artificial Rococo art. For in the mentality of the Enlightenment, the public of amateurs, learned and unlearned, prized individuality and originality as related to the nature and the natural rights of man.

These concepts pervaded values and practice in life before they appeared widely in connection with art. In one of those provocative lags in time between the formulation of ideas by intellectuals and their general acceptance, the word "individuality" was not widely used until about 1760. Although philosophers had written since the Renaissance about the integrity of the ego, expansion of ideas of the worth of the ordinary individual in the eighteenth century encouraged a belief in his right and ability to determine his own destiny. Their wider dissemination coincided with the tip in the balance of real power to the segment of society which controlled its purse strings and which prevailed through individual effort rather than hereditary prerogatives—symptoms of the eroding of the old order years before its institutional supports crumbled.

Lest we become too parochial in our attachment to Western civilization, we should pause for a moment and observe that artists were concerned with such notions as originality and novelty as long ago as 2000 B.C. An Egyptian author of the Twelfth Dynasty mused, "Would that I had words that are unknown, utterances and sayings in a new language, that hath not yet passed away, and without that which hath been said repeatedly—not an utterance that hath grown stale, what the ancestors have already said." [8]

Resurgence of old ideas and the possibilities of their implementation depend on particular historical circumstances. Not until the second half of the seventeenth century was the concept of originality sufficiently developed in France to evoke the invention of a new word. It was not, however, at first employed to refer to art. Appearing around 1690, the word "originality" in the eighteenth century accompanied the development of the prejudice in favor of that which "distinguishes" and was used in the context of ideas about the "natural" man. "We should strive to discover what is natural to ourselves," said La Rochefoucauld, "and not to depart from the area of personal authenticity." [9]

The assertion of the worth of the ordinary individual and of emotionality, which transcended social strata, was in fact implemented earlier in an art closer to nature than was painting—landscape gardening. English writers of the first half of the eighteenth century believed that the clipping of trees, as in the geometric forms of French landscaping, was analogous to the regulation of human impulses by social or traditional influences. In the serpentine paths and artfully contrived "natural" growths of English picturesque landscape gardening, men created an art in which they could actually live in simulation of an existence unfettered by the artificialities of civilization. Paradoxically, while English landscaping seemed closer to nature, it was actually patterned after the paintings of Claude Lorrain: "picturesque" was not distinguished from "pictorial" until about 1740. It became a fashionable pastime to walk or travel about the country in coaches, viewing scenery through a convex "Claude glass" which poetically softened the harshness of nature, or simply to loll on the grass, as Wright of Derby painted Sir Brooke Boothby in 1781, reading Rousseau.[10]

In terms of the evolution of words and ideas, landscape, romanticism, and stress on the worth of all men seemed to go together. Particularly after 1750, the term "romantic" was extensively used in England and France in connection with the "picturesque" or quaint in landscape and with what is most individual and almost incommunicable in the impressions we receive from it. Le Tourneur specified that for a landscape to be romantic as well as picturesque, the imagination must "people it with interesting scenes, forgetting the little valley to delight in the ideas and images it has inspired." [11] In the second half of the century also, a fad for exotic styles of architecture in their natural setting blossomed in Walpole's Gothic villa Strawberry Hill and Chambers' Chinese Pagoda in Kew Gardens. Men seemed to be seeking a new relationship to nature.

Like "the natural," "individuality," and "originality," the term "romantic" was applied to the attributes of persons before it designated an art style. In 1789 Frenchmen were using it to signify unique qualities of human beings—ineffable and sudden emotions, spontaneity, imagination—before social influences changed their "natural" feelings.[12]

Not only was this the Age of Sentiment; it was also the Age of Reason. Another aspect of respect for nature held that reason as a universal element never carries man far from what is natural. A rationalistic conception of individualism in uniformity became the basis of the religion of nature which replaced the belief in a supernatural order among many advanced thinkers, including Voltaire and some of the English Deists. Even Rousseau, who found the source of the religion of nature in "the heart" rather than in the reason, wrote, "The worship God requires is that of the heart; and when this is sincere, it is always uniform." [13]

While Rousseau's ideas encouraged individual differentiation, Neoclassicists stressed the element of uniformity and believed that individuals are fundamentally alike. In the distinction between universals and particulars that goes back to Plato, Neoclassicists followed the postulate of an ideal, correct type, a universal and necessary beauty by which individual instances should be judged. David tried to achieve in his art the *beau idéal* he believed the ancients had realized and the moderns should seek.

But the great Neoclassicists did not believe in following their ideal types slavishly, and certainly they were "individualists" who developed highly personal styles which did not exclude particularity. In fact, there was a rage for authenticity of setting and detail as never before within

he context of idealism. But all seemed under the rule of Reason in this
rt where the type prevailed over the particularities that adorned it.
Neoclassicists also depicted intense emotions in their paintings. And they
onsidered that enthusiasm and emotionality on the part of the artist
vere indispensable ingredients in the creation of art. Even admirers
riticized Vien for lacking "the sentiment and energy, the enthusiasm
nd divine fire that should animate the painter and the poet." [14]

However, Neoclassicists, following principles formulated by the
French Academy in the seventeenth century, did not conceive of emotion
s a quality that should emanate freely from the individual painter to
ominate the work of art. Although one of the major categories of
cademic instruction was "expression," the academicians and the clas-
icists thought that a few recipes were the proper means of stating the
isible manifestations of that stable species, Mankind.[15]

The assumptions on which Neoclassicists based their practice hindered
hem from developing landscape painting, which focused attention on the
onstant shiftings rather than on the constants of nature. Although there
vas a group of classicistic landscapists (some of the works of Valen-
iennes in the 1780s remind one of the Roman landscapes Corot painted
fty years later), few pure landscapes, devoid of extraneous allusions,
ccur in the works of Neoclassicists. David painted only one landscape,
nd that while in prison for his connection with Robespierre. Landscape
erved primarily as a backdrop for his pupils during the Empire.

Because it drew attention to changes in nature, landscape painting
vas more closely related to experimental procedures than to relatively
xed typology. The notion of transforming nature in accordance with
nan's desires, which was deeply rooted in the Renaissance and imple-
nented in elaborate landscape gardening, was accentuated by the burst
f scientific experiment and speculation that accompanied the commercial
nd military exploits of the seventeenth century. Empiricism was not
ntipathetic to art in general nor to landscape in particular, for both
cience and art seek to understand and even to rival or surpass nature.
ndeed, landscape painting came into its own in European art during
hat landmark era of Western science, the seventeenth century. How-
ver, at that time, with such vivid exceptions as many of the works of
Hercules Seghers and Jacob von Ruisdael, a classical or Biblical theme
r, in Holland, a more worldly subject, even if overshadowed by ex-
anses of trees, hills, sky or sea, was still generally the excuse for the

existence of the picture. Not until the second half of the eighteenth century, in the works of Richard Wilson and Thomas Girtin, was landscape painted on a wide scale for the purpose of conveying a feeling or emotion inherent in the artist's reactions to it.

Thus landscape painting did not become a major category until the greater prominence of the conception of art in which the feeling of the artist supersedes reason. A different proportioning of reason and feeling was necessary in order for both landscape and Romantic painting to come into their own. David's belief that "the genius in the arts should not have any other guide than the torch of reason" [16] resulted in minimal articulation of individualized feelings in his art. In reversal of the classical rule that the work should be purged of subjective forces which were indispensable during its development, feeling became the definition of art. "The language of the heart is the only one that is universal," Constable said. "Painting is with me but another word for feeling." [17]

There were many guises for the feelings. A painter could still find a ready market, and even a larger one than in the eighteenth century by exploiting feeling in terms of sentimentality. Particularly in England where the Puritanical strain inhibited appreciation of many types of art, paintings of easy and warm association, full of common sense and human interest and reminiscent of keepsake art, were increasingly popular as the Victorian Age became established. Artists even exploited in a maudlin way the side effects of the Industrial Revolution in such paintings as *The Seamstress,* of which a critic wrote in 1844, "Who can help exclaiming, 'Poor Soul! God help her!' If any circumstances could make me wage war against the present social arrangements, and make us go down shirtless to our graves, it is the contemplation of this truthful and wonderful picture." Sentimentalization went so far that Thackeray attacked the insipidity and "milk-and-water of human kindness" of this art.[18]

Not all "realistic" art was so bland. A sharper, even acrid realism recalling Hogarth, entered the works of Daumier, Balzac and Dickens. Due to the spread of lithography in the first forty years of the nineteenth

entury and the greatly increased circulation of newspapers, it could be
disseminated even more widely than in Hogarth's time. The new journalism encouraged the reproduction of scenes from everyday life by such
artists as the Johannot brothers and Achille Devéria, and caricatural
comments on this life by Daumier and Grandville.

By the middle of the nineteenth century, "realism" had become such
a sweeping label of admiration, embracing so many different concepts,
as did Romanticism, that one could scarcely identify it distinctly. Ingres,
that eighteenth-century idealist whose distorted forms had been attacked
by some critics in his youth as ugly and *gothique* and who then was
mistakenly identified with the Romantics, was praised in terms of prevailing realistic criteria. His former pupil Amaury Duval went so far
as to say, with descriptive and historical inaccuracy, "I firmly believe
that M. Ingres, in leading art back to a more faithful accent on nature,
has overthrown the school of David, and has caused the birth of that
evolution of realism which flows over us today." [19] Delacroix, however,
regarded David as a "singular composite of realism and the ideal," which
made him "the father of the whole modern school." He complained that
in the art of Ingres, which was being misused as a model in the pastiche
of academic art, "effort and pretension are everywhere; there is not a
mark of naturalness in it." [20]

Both Duval and Delacroix were trying to reconcile their esteem for
elevation and observation. Regardless of the emotional impact of particular words under the pressure of time and circumstance, no necessary
contradiction between realism and idealism existed, for idealism seeks
to harmonize contradictory qualities in one form which realism pretends
merely to record in their multiplicity. The multiplicity in Romanticism
was, however, quite different. The intrusion into the foreground of the
feelings of the individual led to expectations of greater originality than
in the supposed objectivity of the realists, and greater diversity than
in the limited number of types in Neoclassicism from David to Ingres.

As the uses for painting became more ambiguous, its psychological
function became more explicit, and the role of the artist's feelings and

psyche assumed greater importance in the work of art. Extending idea
that had germinated in the seventeenth century, Delacroix believed tha
"the scientist's personality is absent from his work," while "it is quit
a different matter with the artist. The seal that he imprints on hi
production is what makes it the work of an artist." Thus he admire
Haydon as "a very great talent" but regretted the "absence of a stron
personal style." [21] Fellow artists thought it to be the great fault o
Hugo's protégé Boulanger that, although "he possesses several of th
qualities which go into the making of a great painter, he does not kno
how to be himself." [22]

Originality was accompanied by hazards. A friend wrote to Constabl
when, at the age of thirty-five, he still had not sold a single landscap
that he would have fared better if he had copied more, if he had not ha
"that dread of being a mannerist, and that desire of being an original.
Constable nevertheless continued to cultivate his belief that "the genuir
productions of art, like those of nature, are all distinct from each othe
Every truly original picture is a separate study . . . so that what
right in one, would be often entirely wrong if transferred to another."
Although the persistence of older ideas about the artist and personali
in general helped delay the fuller development of the idea of art as sel
expression until a later date, painting, after a long existence as the pi
turing of expressions, was launched on the road to Expressionism in th
artist's exploration of human feelings, including his own.

A new idealization emerged of artist-creators as "complete men
according to Baudelaire, "those in whom reflection does not kill th
expression of passion." [24] The Romantics did not, however, renoun
controls and reason in creation. As emotionality in art was exploit
over the years by persons who Delacroix believed misunderstood its ro
and used it as a mode of attracting attention, he insisted irritably th
art is not "what the vulgar think it to be, that is, some sort of inspirati
which comes from nowhere, which proceeds by chance, and presents
more than the picturesque externals of things. It is reason itself, adorn
by genius, but following a necessary course and encompassed by high
laws." [25] Although the dual intellectual and emotional views operati
since the Renaissance continued to exist, there was no question as
which was predominant in Romanticism.

The stress on the role of the feelings of the individual encourag

reater focus on the inner world, when the precise study and rendering
f the outer world had been carried farther than ever before. Very few
rtists at this time were ready to go as far as Blake who declared, "The
ature of my Work is Visionary or Imaginative. . . . He who does not
magine in stronger and better lineaments and in stronger and better
ght than his perishing and mortal eyes can see, does not imagine at all.
he painter of the work asserts that all his imagination appear to him
finitely more perfect & more minutely organized than anything seen
this mortal eye."

However, there was a general relaxation, and sometimes a reversal,
the classical doctrine that the realm of the imagination is not the
ay to the truth, but a source of delusions. Dreamlike, even fantastic,
ctures, which were painted by James Barry, Fuseli, and Blake in
ngland in the late eighteenth century, later were commissioned from
rench artists by Napoleon and his retainers. These were not necessarily
manations from or "expressions" of the artist's inner life, but a continu-
ion of the vogue for fantasy in art, dating from the sixteenth century
d perhaps stimulated anew by the late eighteenth-century interest in
e occult.

Girodet advised his pupils to prefer the bizarre to the dull, advice he
llowed himself in *The Paradise of Ossian.* The strange transparencies
this picture may actually have been inspired by the phantasmagoria
ntern, invented in 1802.[26] But his former teacher David was horrified,
claiming, "Oh my! Is Girodet mad? He is mad, or I don't understand
ything about the art of painting: he has created personages of crystal.
ith all his wonderful talent, he will never produce anything but
nsense; he has no common sense." [27]

In French Romantic paintings a quarter of a century later, a greater
oportion of fantasy became artistic doctrine. Admiring the paintings
Decamps in the Salon of 1831, Heine wrote, "The idea of a work
art is born of the emotions or feelings, and this demands of free, wild
ncy the aid of realization." [28] Years after he had spun fancies with the
hograph crayon of *Hamlet* and *Faust* (which Goethe praised highly)
elacroix still maintained, "The finest products of the arts are those
ich express the pure fantasy of the artist." [29] Painters also explored
normal mental states of subjects bearing the impersonality of automata,
e Delacroix's *Convulsionnaires de Tangiers,* and the intense, lonely

realm of the mad in Géricault's series of portraits of the insane and Delacroix's *Tasso in the Madhouse.*

Artists exploited unusual mental states and used "pure fantasy" not only as interesting subject matter but, more deliberately and self-consciously than ever, as ingredients in the inception and execution of the work of art. At the beginning of his career, Delacroix described his source of inspiration in terms that suggest twentieth-century formulations of the unconscious: "There is an old leaven, a black depth that demands satisfaction." Some fifteen years later, he expatiated on the same theme: Painting is the art "from which we receive those mysterious shocks which our soul, freed, as it were, from terrestrial bonds and withdrawn into its most immaterial essence, receives almost unconsciously." [30] With the loosening of outer stringencies on the new art, the artist was freer to exploit these states than formerly—and with the passage of time, it was increasingly expected that he do so in order to be considered modern or avant-garde.

With all their interest in self-expression, some of the most advanced painters were also concerned about the problem of the expressiveness of art for their contemporaries and, at least implicitly, with the idea of art as expressive of the world as well as of the person. In part, this idea was related to the rhetorical tradition that treated the language of art as independent of the individual. In part, it was related to the Renaissance notion that art was an index to the greatness of an age. Putting the artist in the mainstream of history and among the community of fine minds, this belief had contributed to the greater separation of Art from the applied art of the artisan.[31] In the 1820s, when the separation of artists from the mainstream of society as well as from the status of artisan had become more extreme, a favorite slogan was *Il faut être de son temps.*[32]

A complete severance from tradition was not easy, for in art as in society and the lives of individuals, the past dies hard and perhaps never completely. Yet Delacroix, who practiced the lessons of the Renaissance and Baroque masters so extensively, believed, "It is necessary to use the means familiar in the time when you are living, otherwise you will not be understood and you will not live." Though he wrote, "All the great problems of art were solved in the sixteenth century," [33] nevertheless, he and other painters posed new problems which they bequeathed to future generations.

The most striking and controversial effects of the new stress on individual feeling and fantasy were on form and technique, rather than on theme. Subject to more intimate and therefore to multiple interpretations, the new procedures acted as a barrier to communication with the public and even with other artists working in the same vein.

In contrast with Romantic art, both the technique and the content of realistic art seemed to convey facts directly and explicitly. In the vogue for "realism" lay admiration for an imitation of appearances so exact as to deceive the beholder. Reminiscent of similar tales among the ancient Greeks was the story that James Howe's painting of a horse fooled even the horse. Artists, however, would only fool themselves if they believed that in painting "realistic" pictures they were simply setting down nature as presented to the eye. For in accord with a process that characterizes perception in life as well as in art, painters create through sets of mind or points of view that may be submerged or present in awareness which they have acquired from life experiences and from other art.[34]

Even realistic art like Howe's and Meissonier's was based on an elaborate set of illusionistic methods that had been studiously developed in the Renaissance. In the fifteenth and sixteenth centuries, naturalism had culminated in *sfumato* which tamed the intangibilities of nature. It was transformed further in the emotionalized pigment of Rembrandt, the atmospheric effects of Velásquez, and the all-over flicker of the Rococo. The essentially vague and ambiguous seemed to become definite in the Neoclassical schema of clear definition, shallow space, and smooth finish, making something concrete of the eighteenth-century conception of the *beau idéal,* based not on observation of natural phenomena but on the application of *a priori* principles.

The Neoclassicists thought to clarify and ennoble their works by means of simple forms and compositions, which they often associated with primitive and therefore higher phases of civilization, going back from the Romans to the Greeks. Simplicity and sobriety were sometimes cultivated even by an artist like Fragonard, whom we know for his Rococo works, when he sought the financial rewards of official commis-

sions. Thus in *Croesus and Callirhoe,* hailed as a masterpiece in 176
he placed between two columns with no distracting ornament the trag
group of the priest sacrificing himself rather than his beloved.[35] Accor
ing to Delécluze, David thought that by avoiding complex scenes
painter could maintain unity, controlling the attention of the observe
and instructing in duty or virtue. Sometimes Neoclassicists restricted th
observer's imagination through use of drapery that cuts the figures in th
picture off from the background space.

At the same time, however, a tendency to excite the imagination wa
present in the official revival of seventeenth-century art. Diagonal ge
tures are the keynotes of Vincent's *President Molé;* and in Ménageot
Death of Leonardo da Vinci (1781), the deathbed extends not on
horizontal plane as in contemporary Neoclassical deathbed scenes, bu
into the picture space. In distracting and complex composition and i
their attempts at historical accuracy, these works are more than a reviva
of the Baroque; they suggest the Romantic painting of the future.

As different as Romantic painters were among themselves (this c
course was true also of Neoclassicists), they exhibit some of the sam
general norms of style. Although Delacroix's expressive vehicle is th
human figure and that of Turner and Constable, landscape, their work
have in common a lack of closed outlines. These artists sought movemen
in depth through the use of diagonals, overlappings, asymmetry, mu
tiplicity of planes, and interpenetration of bright color, light and a
mosphere, or dramatic chiaroscuro. When traditional classicistic elemen
are used, they are changed to fit a new taste for indeterminateness in ar
The triangle, a containing motif of repose for Raphael and for h
nineteenth-century admirer Ingres, becomes a thing of wavy and pen
trable boundaries for Delacroix.

While the Romantics tried to heighten an effect of illusion, they di
not direct it so strongly as the artists of the Baroque. Romantic figu
works, no matter how animated, convey a feeling of incomplete actio
and tenseness, rather than of tension released, as in the Baroque. I
general, the mood of Romantic art, as contrasted with Neoclassical,
emotionalized, whether as physical activation or introspection.

Because of its contrast with Neoclassical moods and patterns, Roman
tic art was often attacked as formless, not only in painting but also i
music. Thus Beethoven was slow to be received in France because h
works were thought to ignore barbarously the laws of compositio

Delacroix, however, wrote, "Beethoven moves us . . . because he is the man of our time. He is romantic to the supreme degree." [36]

Even a style of formlessness is simply another kind of form. Actually, both Romantic and Neoclassical works were carefully composed. In fact, some of Delacroix's art is too obviously, almost compulsively composed, as in *Jacob Wrestling with the Angel,* in which a painfully prominent arrow in the foreground points as in a twentieth-century advertisement to the main item of interest. However, paintings that were more completely Romantic in style functioned in terms of which Burke had written before the French Revolution, "Confused, obscure, uncertain images have on the imagination more of the force which produces grand passions than clearer and more definite images."

In visual art, this involved certain uses of lines, colors, and shapes which are the elements of painting as letters and words are of literature and as tones and rhythms are of music. The meanings and impact of these elements, however, as employed in complex works of art, are not constant and universal but depend on time and circumstance. Thus, while color was the chief vehicle of Romantic painting, it was developed earlier and was carried further in England, though not necessarily in connection with Romantic tendencies.

French painters tended to associated dominance of line with academicism. While a Frenchman might feel hemmed in by a stress on outline, the opposite might be true for an English painter. For in England color rather than line was associated with academic practice, stemming from the style Van Dyck had introduced in court circles in the seventeenth century. Opposing the grand manner toward which Sir Joshua Reynolds directed official taste, Blake deplored the "ooze," the technique of chiaroscuro which brings about "that the execution shall be all blocked up with brown shadows." Although he had seen few paintings by old masters, he eulogized Raphael and Michelangelo but condemned painters who, he supposed, had influenced moderns whom he disliked. Among the masters he so blindly rejected were Titian and Rubens—those "Venetian and Flemish Demons," to be so warmly admired by French Romantics, who "cause that everything in art shall become a Machine." In the Descriptive Catalogue to his unsuccessful exhibition of 1809, he mystically declaimed, "The great and golden rule of art, as well as life, is this: That the more distinct, sharp, and wirey the bounding line, the more perfect the work of art. . . ." [37] While Blake used line as his expressive vehicle, the wiry style in which he pretended to transcribe things from the realm of his imagination bears little resemblance to the soft and elegant undulations of his friend John Flaxman's silhouettes that idealized classical forms.

Not simply an emphasis on line itself, but a certain kind of line characterizes the type of style. The Romantics, of course, were also preoccupied with drawing. Delacroix believed his drawings so important that he never parted with them; he even worked out a plan by which they were to be classified after his death.

The contours of Romantic drawings are often jagged or open, like the composition of the paintings, permitting the surrounding page or canvas to elide with the interior of the contours, much as color and chiaroscuro bring ground and figure into closer contact. The drawings of Neoclassicists, on the other hand, like the composition of their paintings in turn, are closed. Yet even within a closed contour style, the quality of line itself produces a different over-all effect. Ingres' contours are undulating, not rigid as with David's, almost in keeping with the serpentine line that Hogarth had made the basis of his theory of art: yet two more different artists than Hogarth and Ingres cannot be imagined. Flaxman, Hogarth's countryman of the next generation, also excelled in the use of the serpentine line, though in his hands it ceased to be ebullient. Where serpentine binding lines occur in Neoclassical works, they are not dramatic. For example, in Flaxman's sculpture *Come, Thou Blessed,* the group of angels assisting Miss Cromwell to heaven shapes the form of an arabesque but lacks the verve of the sweeping arabesques of Delacroix's *Abduction of Rebecca.*

Despite their differences, it is not at all surprising that Romantics admired the works of Neoclassicists, particularly in the earlier days of their movement before extraneous factors intervened, for artists value fine works which may be quite different from their own. Sympathy or difference of taste and style does not necessarily imply that the things liked or disliked belong to the same or to different orders. While they are at their peak, art styles are not so well defined as they become at a later date; autopsy awaits their decline and death. Only in retrospect does the expression of anti-Romantic and pro-Classical sentiments by even the greatest French Romantic painter, Delacroix, seem to be a paradox of history or of this particular man. It is, rather, characteristic of the ambivalence of the human mind, which reconciles conflicts into that style of behavior and inner life we call "personality."

Nevertheless, a confusion in meaning and terminology persists. "Form" is often said to be the chief interest of the classical artist, subject matter of the romantic—even to the extent of overwhelming form. Critics, however, have defined both classicism and romanticism in terms of form. Some writers claim that the "classicism" of David is followed first by the "proto-baroque" of Prud'hon and Gros, then by the "romantic late classicism" of Ingres, by the "early Baroque with realistic tendencies" of Géricault, and by the "romantic high Baroque" of Delacroix. Others have called Delacroix a "classic romantic." [38]

Though an art style, like a personality, can be analyzed into its countless modalities, it is not their sum total, but a rubric of their interworkings. There is no such thing as a "pure" style; a single style may admit the intrusion of elements from other styles while preserving its over-all quality intact.

Elements of different styles may enter into the works of a given artist, though they cannot be isolated to designate a particular style. Ingres' work, more svelte and sensuous than the classicism of the previous generation, nevertheless belongs to the same artistic norm as that of David, of which it is a survival. Two of the greatest artists of the early nineteenth century, Blake and Corot, used some of the elements of Neoclassicism, but we cannot convincingly think of them as Neoclassicists. Although Blake stressed the outline, a trademark of the Neoclassicists, we do not feel the same over-all quality in Blake and Neoclassical work. And though perceptual space and atmosphere are virtually absent from his art, his preoccupation with the imagination and feeling of the individual make him seem closer to the Romantics. After the 1840s, Corot painted in both his styles. The mist-dissolved masses of trees in the forest scenes are far removed from his Italian landscapes of the 1820s and 1830s, where strong sunlight shapes the quiet blocks of buildings and rocks. He developed his evanescent style when the solidity of Neoclassicism and Realism was deeply entrenched in public taste.

The concrete, naturalistic image in art was threatened as never before by developments that culminated a century later in its obliteration in abstract painting. This destruction and new construction were rooted in a conception of naturalism not in terms of externals, but in the sense of the inner realities of men and nature. Alfred de Musset, though famous as a writer, recalled in his *Confession d'un enfant du siècle,* "I studied painting. There, doubtless, in that plastic art, which is concerned only with lines and colors, the truth would have to appear to me." Even Delacroix, so addicted to literary subjects, mused, "Painting does not always need a subject." [39]

The dissolution of the naturalistic image began with a different employment of paint in the creation of the painting. Departing from the academic practice of mixing colors with black, which dulled the "molecules" of colors and produced tones that "no longer play," [40] Delacroix achieved a stronger play of gray through complementary colors, using pure pigments instead of mixtures in some areas of the canvas. Through the years, he learned about color and atmosphere from various artistic sources, as well as from his own studies of nature. He observed that the green in the grasses of Constable's work is composed of a multitude of different greens carrying an intensity and vivacity which are lacking when a uniform tint or only different values are used. This method conveys the scintillating effect of objects in the open air. In the 1830s, in the brilliant colors and the bright sunlight of North Africa, he received further stimulation for the coloristic ideas he had already absorbed from a spectrum of paintings—the works of Velásquez, Rubens, Goya, Gros, Géricault, Bonington, and Constable.

In a renewal of the old dispute over the relative merits of line and color that descended from the Florentines and the Venetians in the Renaissance and from the Poussinistes and the Rubénistes in the seventeenth century, Delacroix and other Romantics were attacked for their use of stronger pigments. Many Frenchmen of the first half of the nineteenth century regarded color as a metaphor for moral judgments or values in life quite outside art. During the 1820s when Romantic painters were exploiting color as an integral part of artistic style and Eugène Devéria was hailed as the "French Veronese," a vogue for the word "color" invaded popular speech (Balzac said the public wanted "de la couleur"). But this vogue did not necessarily extend to art, at least not for all of the public.

Line was often opposed to color as a more spiritual element, a reversal of the medieval idea of color as divine illumination. Lamennais wrote in 1840, "Where color is the principal preoccupation of the artist, art will tend to be material; there will be, on the contrary, a tendency to be spiritual if the artist occupies himself mainly with drawing; color should be subordinated to drawing, otherwise sensation will prevail over thought and art will be humbled." [41] Ingres' subdued use of pigment was a positive attraction for those who thought color to be a materialistic and earthly element.

Delacroix and Constable did not, however, conceive of color primarily as an excitant for the senses, but as a compositional element. When critics complained of Constable's work, "Not an inch of repose is to be found anywhere. Plants, foliage, sky, timber, stone—everything—all are contending for individual notice," they mistook for disunity what was actually a kind of unity based on atmosphere rather than on geometrical construction or grand compositional arabesques. Corot, Rousseau, and Huet also became increasingly interested in a semihomogeneous atmosphere and surface texture, utterly removed from the clearly defined color areas and smooth surfaces of Neoclassical works, creating paintings in which mists, as in Romantic poetry, are more important than outlines.[42]

The most advanced artists of the time were engrossed by the effects of an unfinished quality and the creative use of the accidental, as a means of capturing the immediacy of experience or the fleeting aspects of nature. Thus Constable wrote to his future biographer Leslie in 1833 of his desire to render the qualities of "light-dews-breezes-bloom-and-freshness . . . not one of which has yet been perfected on the canvas of any painter in the world." To twentieth-century eyes accustomed to more extreme shorthand allusions to nature in art, the canvases of Constable, attacked by contemporaries as too sketchy, look very "finished"; on the other hand, we prize his oil sketches as finished paintings. But in his day, the unexpected spots and impasto seemed crude beside the polished or carefully careless strokes perfected by the Academicians. Even paintings based on numerous preliminary studies, such as *The Hay Wain,* disturbed many viewers because of their "unfinished quality."

The creative use of the accidental was not a new idea. In the first century A.D., Pliny had extolled the role of chance in the inventions of art, and during the Renaissance Alberti, Vasari, and scores of artists in

The National Gallery, London. Reproduced by courtesy of the Trustees

Constable, *The Hay Wain*, 1821

The National Gallery, London. Reproduced by courtesy of the Trustees

Constable, *The Hay Wain* (detail)

studios discussed and praised the unfinished. In the sixteenth century, Michelangelo's last unfinished sculptures were highly valued as being closer to the artist's psychic life—and this not in an elite circle but in a guidebook to Florence. Sketchiness of execution in painting and in drawing, which made visible the process of creation, occurred in Tintoretto and the late Titian, and was fairly widespread in the seventeenth century, most memorably in Velásquez, Rembrandt and Hals, and in the inauguration of a style of improvisation with the invention of caricature.[43]

During the Renaissance, an unfinished quality in art was often associated with a nonchalance of manner marking the perfect courtier and the perfect artist, as the opposite of the finish that was associated with work of the lowly artisan. This social-aesthetic idea spread with the growth of an amateur public in the early eighteenth century. As if echoing Leonardo and forecasting Rorschach, the painter Alexander Cozens in the 1780s wrote a book advocating the use of accidental ink blots for the suggestion of landscape motifs by the aspiring amateur.

Increasing interest in the use of unfinished, accidental, spontaneous elements in art was associated with the new attitudes to nature that developed in the eighteenth century. Improvements in transportation within both England and France may have had further effects on art. The increase in coach travel in the 1820s and 1830s, when railroads were still in their infancy, encouraged outings and trips through the countryside and, by putting the vision of the artist and the spectator in closer touch, helped spread a taste for paintings of landscape and local interest. Bonington's joy was to travel about France making sparkling sketches in watercolor of seacoast, landscape, and Gothic monuments. Corot and other painters, including his friends of the Barbizon group, wandered leisurely through the countryside sketching, untroubled by the noise and smoke of iron horses. Although *plein air* painting, in which the finished work was actually done on the spot, had to wait for the Impressionists, these earlier painters established the custom of observing, contemplating, and sketching nature on the spot, on a greater scale than in the past. As Girtin, Constable, and Turner had recently done in England, the French artists also studied the shifting and flickering of light in nature, capturing its effects around the same time that photography began to do so.

Artistic exploration of light and movement did not become obsolete with the rapid development of photography in the 1830s and 1840s. On the contrary, the camera freed painters from the extreme literalness of so much mid-century art which seemed to vie with photography. Constable's cloudscapes and his studies of changing atmospheric effects at different times of day, Turner's *Rain, Steam, and Speed—the Great Western Railway* in 1837 and *Shade and Darkness, Light and Color,* and *Steamer in a Snowstorm* in 1842 were preludes to the Impressionists' studies of evanescent atmospheric elements that formerly had been only auxiliaries in painting—even though they threatened to take over the field of interest as early as Rembrandt, Caravaggio, and Velásquez.

Of course, the finished works of many of the greatest artists came to appear obsolete to the eyes of later generations, while sketches—which, like many portraits and other intimate paintings, they had intended only for themselves or friends—are highly prized. It is therefore not surprising that some of the exhibition pieces of even so outstanding a painter as Delacroix look stale today. In fact, though his use of color led him to be attacked very early in his career, Delacroix never realized his theoretical ideas in practice as fully as some other painters of the early nineteenth century. Not only personal factors were responsible. For it was more difficult for a figure painter than for a landscapist to use the new ideas consistently. As a newer type, pure landscape painting held fewer inhibitions than figure painting, associated with long-established conventions. Moreover, the advanced techniques would entail a semidissolution of the image of the human body which was, psychologically speaking, a much more drastic step to take.

As the traditional uses for painting declined, many artists found less virtue in old practices and training. Deploring the dissemination of careless technique, Delacroix feared that the tradition of the old masters was "completely lost. Bad products, negligence in the preparations, canvases, brushes, abominable oils, lack of care on the part of the artist. . . . David introduced this negligence through his affectation of contempt for the material means."[44] Thus a preoccupation with the spiritual and ideological function of painting often accorded less importance to the technical skills that had been hallowed for centuries. Indeed, many artists and art lovers, like the positivist Auguste Comte, believed that art school instruction stifles the aesthetic impulse.[45] Instead of spending long years of apprenticeship or studying in the official academy or in the studio of a master, many young French painters of the 1820s and 1830s studied only a short time in an atelier before exhibiting their pictures. Others rebelled against all training and went to study by themselves in the museums.[46] It was a common complaint that artists were neglecting the technical aspect of their art. Particularly bitter was Gros's attack on the Romantics at Girodet's funeral where, between tears and sobs, he cried, "Soon they will have us believe that a bit of canvas on which color has been daubed for two weeks is a masterpiece."[47] Even a careful composer like Delacroix believed that "execution, in painting, should always have about it something of improvisation."[48]

The idea recurs in the early nineteenth century that a casualness and directness of appearance, and even imperfections and accidents in painting, are approximations of nature and of natural spontaneity, and a route to the most basic elements of creative experience. Some artists, including Géricault and Delacroix, extended eighteenth-century ideas of "original" childhood, unspoiled by the pressures of the world. They believed that the simple, primitive sort of view that characterizes children makes possible a freshness which stales under instruction. Corot advised, "It is necessary to interpret nature with naïveté and according to your personal feeling, detaching yourself completely from what you know from old masters or contemporaries. In that way alone will you succeed in moving. . . . Every day I pray God to make me a child again, that is, to see Nature without preoccupations and to render it like a child." [49]

The kind of simplicity these artists had in mind was diametrically opposed to that of the Neoclassicists who sought the primitive not within the human being, but in earlier phases of high civilization. Although many critics in the mid-nineteenth century found Ingres' work "archaic" because of its simple forms which contrasted with the elaborate eclecticism of the time, this simplicity and primitivism were not elemental. Neoclassical archaism was highly sophisticated, related not to the simplicity of line and space as, for instance, in Quattrocento art, but to such elegant austerity as the neo-Palladian vogue among early eighteenth-century aesthetes in the English aristocracy and the finesse of the decorative art of the Adam brothers.

The Romantics and their partisans accused the Neoclassicists who were active in the 1840s of being too artificial. Baudelaire criticized Ingres for "an almost morbid preoccupation with style," and praised Decamps who "loves to capture nature in the very act, in her simultaneous movements of fantasy and reality—in her most sudden and most unexpected aspects." [50]

However, an appearance of spontaneity and naturalness can be merely another convention. Rococo art effects that type of naturalness which pertains not to nature or the elemental, but to a kind of apparent spontaneity analogous in social life to the grace which Castiglione had specified for the courtier and which became an accoutrement of the dandy. Cultivation of an unfinished quality, especially in the backgrounds, had been a special conceit of English art since the days of Gainsborough and Reynolds, akin to the careful carelessness of the fashionable ladies they painted. Delacroix disliked that sophisticated facility, which was a convention of the English school as it had been in the French Rococo, in the work of Lawrence, Turner, and their "grandfather" Reynolds, because of "the defect of exaggeration, particularly as to the effect, which prevents them from being classed among the great masters." [51]

The Frenchman was himself a master of facility. Baudelaire wrote that Delacroix thought rapidity of execution desirable even in grand studio pieces, that he advised a young painter that he should be able to sketch a man in the time it took him to fall from a fourth-story window if he hoped to be able some day to execute those more ambitious paintings known as "great machines," [52] whose very name suggests the antithesis of the spontaneous.

Even for the Neoclassicist Ingres, ease of execution was the ideal, but it eluded him. He believed, "the greatest task for a good painter is to think about his whole picture, to have it, so to speak, all in his head, in order to execute it quickly and as if all new." In practice, he painted slowly and laboriously, experiencing tremendous anxiety with the monumental works he managed to finish. Difficulties with his masterful, incisive portraits caused him such anguish that he would burst into tears and have to be comforted by the sitter as he cried, "I can't draw anymore; I don't know anything." Ingres rationalized, "the rapidity of execution which is necessary for distinguished color does not accord with the profound study that the purity of great forms requires." [53]

Speed of execution was not an absolutely necessary condition for originality. Whereas Delacroix astonished with his rapidity and worked successively on a dozen paintings, Constable would work long and conscientiously on a single canvas. He spent seven years and many sleepless nights completing *The Opening of Waterloo Bridge*.

Like his process of creating a picture he considered to be completed, Constable's success in achieving general recognition in England was slow. His acceptable subject matter was not sufficient for his pictures to sell widely. Although Joseph Farington, an important member of the Royal Academy, predicted when Constable visited London in 1795 that his style would one day "form a distinct feature in the art," this style did not fit in with either the taste for idealism or realism in painting.

Even urban Englishmen could understand Constable's attachment to "the sound of water escaping from mill-dams, willows, old rotten planks, slimy posts, and brickwork. I love such things . . . and I associate 'my careless boyhood' with all that lies on the banks of the Stour; those scenes made me a painter." [54] To some viewers, however, Constable's pictures looked too sketchy and therefore unrealistic. Finally, beginning in the late 1830s, his paintings began to sell better, as if at last they seemed to fit in with a fashion for cottage art, with its vine-covered walls and contented cows and horses in dewy meadows, that had become standard fare for the parlor. And gradually Constable's pigment which had been ridiculed as "white sky mud" was seen to be, after all, discreet in over-all effect and color, and solid and respectful of objects of the familiar world.

This taste might at first appear to be the "expression" of a world whose mentality had become so "materialistic" that after 1830 *positif* and *confortable* replaced *l'idéal* in ordinary speech.[55] Since materialism respects the concrete, we might expect a decreasing taste for the sketchy or vague during its ascendancy. Actually, the increasingly dematerialized mists of Corot and the shadowy forest fastnesses of Huet, as well as the art of Constable, became more popular after 1840. The public had "learned to see" this art which, like an allegory or a foreign language, required familiarity or knowledge for a sympathetic response.

But if, as is often said, an artist "teaches" the public to see, it is not necessarily true that the public "learns" the same things the artist sees and feels. Constable himself had not thought of his art in terms of literal realism. He pointed out that landscape "was first used as an assistant in conveying sentiment" in the works of Giotto and other early Italians, and in his own work he made it the principal vehicle of feeling, with anecdotal interest subordinate or completely absent.

The "materialistic" atmosphere also fostered a taste for *l'idéal*. Many persons of the newer middle classes, as they became established, had come to wish something grand, in the manner of the old aristocracy whose roles they were assuming—though not so extravagant in treatment as to offend their own limited experience. For these patrons Turner's grandiose settings, dissolving in blazes of color, dazzled the senses and violated commonsensical reality. At the beginning of Victoria's reign in 1837, a critic attacked his use of "a medium of yellow, scarlet and orange, and azure-blue, as only lives in his own fancy and the toleration

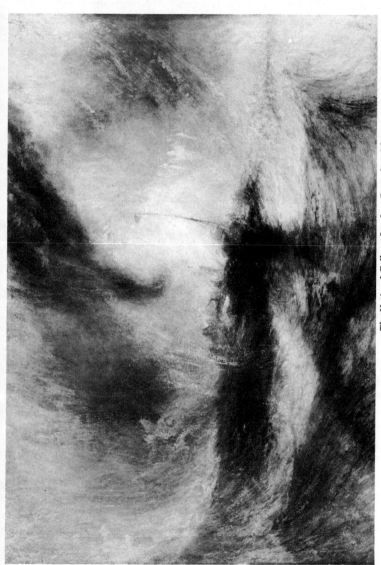

The National Gallery, London. Reproduced by courtesy of the Trustees

Turner, *Steamer in a Snowstorm*, 1842

of his admirers. It is grievous to us to think of talent, so mighty and poetical, running riot into such frenzies." [56] Nevertheless, one of the most sensitive critics of the century defended the artist. Ruskin found visual support in Turner's art for values he feared were being lost in the life of the day. As was the case with his championing of Gothic art and of the arts and crafts movement, his defense in *Modern Painters* (1843) of Turner who "spiritualized everything in the visible world" was for him a defense of spiritual values in general.

On the other hand, Constable explored, long before the Impressionists, to an uncanny degree the effects of natural forces on the visible world. This brought him closer to British empiricist thought, which did not negate the value of the imagination but encouraged the subjective activity and immediate feeling of the individual as a starting point for any investigation. In fact, he defined painting not only as "feeling," but (in a phrase reminiscent of Leonardo) as "a science of which pictures are the experiments." Thus an equivalent though not a simultaneous trend of thought and feeling, based on the dual objective and subjective aspects of British empiricism, provided a substratum in which a public could find common ground with Constable at a time it needed a poetic experience, in its own terms, as an accompaniment and, at least unconsciously, as an antidote to those other offspring of empiricism—utilitarianism, technology, and science.

Constable's "experiments" were not, therefore, impersonal works of the laboratory. Even in these landscapes where human beings seldom appear except as tiny spots, man was not displaced from art but was more than ever before involved in it. For this type of painting placed greater demands on his personal experience. As painting became more overtly the record of an artistic or creative experience, rather than a "purely" visual matter, it required greater participation from the spectator and, at the same time, concentrated more attention on the artist's personality and style of life as related to his style of art.

FIVE

Style in Art & Life

The artist himself, painter or writer, often elicited more interest than the work of art. Carlyle wrote in 1827 that the grand question "usual with the best of our own critics at present is a question mainly of a psychological sort, to be answered by discovering and delineating the peculiar nature of the poet from his poetry." [1]

Such a psychological question is not easy to answer. For though, like a poem or a picture, the style of this "peculiar nature" or personality may be sensed as a whole, it is a shimmering network of infinite modalities and meanings. Others experience and define it through a person's behavior. Since a person spends a large part of his life in his work, people often see his nature or personality in terms of the image—visual or conceptual—they have of his occupation. The more of life it involves, as with artists or scientists, the more the character of the person and of his occupation seem to be intertwined.

Not only does an occupation have its specialized skills and economic structure. It also requires or inspires a certain way of life, involving the allocation of time, the extent to which other persons must be pleased or placated, whether one sits, moves about, gets one's hands dirty or dresses elegantly. All these choices and actions define something about the person.

Painters and writers themselves found the exceptional nature of the artist to reside in the nature of his work, which was different from that of other men. In contrast to the mere drudgery of labor or the tedium of a job, the artist's work was endowed with pleasures other men associated with leisure. Balzac, in his *Traité de la vie élégante*, making a tripartite division of society into the classes of the man who works, the man who thinks, and the man who does nothing, found that the artist is the exception, for his work is his rest.

In the close connection between the practical means of life and emotional expression, such a relationship to work encouraged a manner that tended to be different from that of a bookkeeper chained to his ledger, or of a clerk who dons the smile of friendliness, or of a physician or lawyer in the formally structured dealings with patients or clients. However, nonartists might possess some of the attributes associated with artists. Delacroix observed that "one sees certain society people who have the capacity for enjoyment that is found among artists—I use that word to sum up my idea—and who make a great effort to have artists around them, really finding pleasure in their conversation." Regardless of a person's profession, if he displayed intelligence and independence of mind, Delacroix could "promptly pass over the eccentricities" of such a man, grateful for "the unexpected quality of his talk, his artist-quality in everything, which makes of him a precious original." [2]

While some people were charmed by eccentricities, others found them odd and offensive because they seemed to clash with modes of life adhering to more common occupations and to differentiate artists from other men. The artistic process itself separates artists from others. Indeed, artists are more aware of the possibilities of solitude and unusual states of mind, which they use creatively, whereas other men do not give them form and permit them to waste away. Solitude, which is a part of the adult's creative work as it is for the young child absorbed in play, and the deliberate intermittent surrender to the passive, inactive states of reverie and dream, all self-consciously part of the artistic process of many artists, were proscribed in the life of this job-work-success society.

Even for painters like Delacroix whose habits were methodical, their work permitted a greater irregularity of habits—self-determination of working hours and time spent thinking and gazing at flowers or models, and occasionally dabbing and doodling without actually producing any finished work to put on the market. Mme. Celnart, in *The Gentleman and Lady's Book of Politeness,* popular in France and, in translation, in the English-speaking world in the 1830s, asked, "Do artists come under the common rule. . . . Do they live like others—these men . . . passionate, absorbed in thought, ingenuous, almost always strangers to calculation, to pleasure, and to the occupations of this world? No, they have a separate existence, one which the world does not comprehend, and which they ought to conceal from the world." [3]

The artist is ordinary as well as extraordinary. Even if such a stereo-typed individual as described by the authority on etiquette existed, he could not have a separate existence even if he wanted it. For one person simultaneously plays different roles which, in a complex society, may conflict with each other. Even those who are relatively free from rules in their work are nonetheless confronted by regulations in the social world. Not only did artists practice a certain profession; they were born into certain social strata in particular countries and had friends who were not artists. In some areas of his life, therefore, a painter might behave in a way characteristic of persons in those groups rather than of other artists.

The result was a <u>confusion of identities</u> and even of self-iden-tification. With their changing social attachments, artists were forced to find models for a life style elsewhere than in their loosely organized profession. This was also true of the population in general. For the lack of fixed identities was one of the liberating and disturbing con-sequences of the greater fluidity of social strata. Even the common man had at his disposal an historical gallery of ideal types to serve as models for himself and his view of other persons.

A series of portraits illustrates the change in conceptions of how a man should conduct himself. A pastel by Quentin de la Tour—one of his self-portraits, for instance, the head turned with a saucy glance—is an appropriate accompaniment for the world of the eighteenth-century salon. The ideal type was *l'homme vertueux et sensible*—the virtuous and sensitive man of feeling, an affirmation of the Enlightenment's idea of the native goodness of man and of the value of feeling as opposed to restraints on freedom of spirit. At the same time, he conserved the seventeenth-century ideal of the sincere and just gentleman—*l'honnête homme*—with his good sense, finesse, and taste for moderation and order. Along with the man of feeling in the eighteenth century was the *philo-sophe,* the man of reason, who embodied an urge for control and formality and also for graver feelings.[4]

The man of reason was also concerned with the feelings. Diderot believed the emotions of the man of feeling must be passionate, not effervescent or frivolous, and specifically so in art. "Everything which

The Louvre, Paris. Archives photographiques

Géricault, *Portrait of an Artist in His Studio*, ca. 1818-19

passion inspires, I pardon," he wrote before the middle of the century. "I have always been the apologist for strong passions; they alone move me. Arts of genius are born and extinguished with them." [5] In the intent eyes and pressed lips of David's self-portrait of 1794, in the appearance of a strongly willed imposition of control over intense feelings, we can

The Louvre, Paris. Archives photographiques

Ingres, *Portrait of M. Bertin,* 1832

sense the emergence of a new man who would have looked out of place in the eighteenth-century salon or drawing room.

In the parlor or office of the first half of the nineteenth century was to be seen the living image of the Moderate Man of the newly powerful middle class, an embodiment in a less intellectualized aspect of the *philosophes'* double ideal of moderation and passion. A prosperous citizen of the bourgeois monarchy confronts the observer in Ingres' sharp portrait of M. Louis Bertin the Elder. To this painting of a successful bourgeois who appears at once intense, suspicious, and aggressive, we can apply Théophile Silvestre's description of the artist himself: "There he was squarely seated in an armchair, motionless as an Egyptian god carved of granite, his hands stretched wide over parallel knees, his torso stiff, his head haughty." [6] Here the expression of intense feelings was more tensely subjugated than in any "reasonable" man whom Diderot might have admired.

The Romantic portrait exposes the Passionate Man, whether enveloped by his dreams like Géricault's artist in his studio or smoldering with intensity as in Delacroix's portrait of Chopin. What a contrast is *Monsieur Bertin*—the epitome of the man of the "golden mean" which, incubating in the *juste milieu* of the Restoration, had come to prevail as a standard of behavior in France and England. In elaborating and transforming eighteenth-century precepts that moderation is preferable to excess, the Citizen King Louis Philippe made a stereotype of moderation and, in retaliation, was caricatured with his top hat, umbrella, and pot belly as the symbol of dullness, in *Monsieur Poire* by Daumier's employer Philippon.

With the bourgeois victory in 1830, a new period of disquiet began, not so much of discontent on the part *of* the middle class, as in 1789, but of discontent *with* it. Its political battles largely won, the French middle class surrendered the air of noble aspiration it had assumed in 1789 to the competitiveness of daily business enterprise. The new rulers, unlike their counterparts of 1789, did not canalize excitable impulses for the implementation of ideals of liberty, to which they still paid lip service but which they suppressed for the cultivation of a "golden mean." England, with its more liberal political institutions, demonstrated that political and inner personal freedom are not necessarily reciprocal.

In France also, the freedom and individuality which the middle class furthered in business and industry, embodied in the doctrine of laissez-faire, did not extend to the personal emotional life of the individual. Despite the lesser extent of political freedom in the eighteenth century, a greater degree of emotional liberty had existed in the life of the aristocracy, often as libertinage. As the bourgeois in his turn became the overseer of life from his higher and dominating place in the social hierarchy, his more restrictive point of view prevailed. Stendhal expressed an opinion widely held among critics of the new society when he wrote in 1836 in his third preface to *Lucien Leuwen,* "In the Nineteenth Century, democracy, of necessity, introduces the reign of mediocre, rational, narrow-minded and *dull* people." In the eyes of Alexis de Tocqueville, France had become "the land of dumb conformity" half a century after the Revolution he regarded as the most drastic social revolution the world had ever known.

An excess of conformity, however, violated the canon of moderation. Mme. Celnart cautioned the well-bred and those who were making their way up the ladder of the mobile society and wished to appear well-bred, "Moderation in everything is so essential that it is even a violation of propriety itself to affect too much the observance of it." [7] In one of the most popular artists of the time, conformity itself became eccentricity. David Wilkie's touching efforts to act the part of gentleman, accorded by his knighthood, led him to violate the norms of the proper conduct he too assiduously pursued. "His oddity arose from an extreme desire to be exactly like other people," wrote Leslie. "Naturally shy and reserved, he forced himself to talk. . . . Knowing from the station he had acquired he must do such things, he made public speaking a study. He carried the same desire of being correct into lesser things. . . . When quadrilles were introduced, Wilkie, who, like most other people of his rank, had danced reels and country dances, set himself in the most serious manner to study them. His mind was not a quick one and he even drew ground plans and elevations of the new dances to aid his memory." [8]

There remained large numbers of people, not all of them artists, who wanted to be different from their contemporaries. For equality had seemed more attractive when desired than when realized, even though realized only in part. Balzac wrote, "From the moment that . . . the natural son of a millionaire bath-keeper and a man of talent have the same rights as the son of a count, we can no longer be distinguished (sic) except by our intrinsic worth. Thus, in our society, differences have disappeared: there are only nuances."

In the conflict between the ideals of liberty, equality, and individuality that had illuminated the beginnings of the new age, some members of the society of the "golden mean" regarded attempts to actualize the ideal of individuality as conducive to mental pathology. A physician,

Géricault's friend Dr. Georget, wrote in 1823, "The number of insane persons was bound to increase in several countries, because of the development and activity of human faculties which the middle and lower echelons of society have won during the last half century. . . . This sickness is born and increases with circumstances that acutely excite the attention, activate the spirit, and put into play all of men's passions." [9]

In the dullness and emotional repressiveness of the societies of the "golden mean," many spirits craved excitation more than ever. Buffeted on the tides of change, youths embarked on an artistic career upon a wave of vague enthusiasm such as has risen in various forms throughout history—in the children's crusades and the activities of the wandering scholars of the Middle Ages, in the protoreligious air of the French Revolution, in the spasmodic ecstacies of religious sects—among people seeking outlets for their energies. In the early nineteenth century, specific adherence to the standard of art constituted a pledge of loyalty to enthusiasm.

Polite society admonished, in the words of Mme. Celnart, "Let [the artist] reserve only for his friends his noble and striking bursts of inspiration. [Otherwise] people will accuse him of arrogance, of vanity, and perhaps even of madness; for enthusiasm is not included in nor admitted into society." [10] Many artists and art students demonstrated their dissent from these prohibitions by deviating exhibitionistically from the norms of polite society.

Art-student demonstrators were not an innovation of the Romantic period. They followed an old tradition of Bohemian protesters and nonconformists whose descendants in the late eighteenth and early nineteenth century adopted period styles of nonconformity in conduct as well as in art. Their behavior styles paralleled the shift in emphasis in art themes from classical antiquity to the Middle Ages or Renaissance. Moreover, their preoccupation with the mute visual eloquence of bodily expressiveness was a counterpart of an interest in physiognomy already prominent in the eighteenth century among physicians and other writers, notably Fuseli's friend, the Swiss pastor Johann Kaspar Lavater.

Among David's pupils under the Consulate was a small group known as the *barbus, penseurs,* or *primitifs,* who attacked their master for modifying his more severe style. These classicist idealists, in line with the idea common in the eighteenth century that matter mirrors the world and manner mirrors the man, specified their awareness of the emblematic value of outer appearances in terms of dress and demeanor. Led by Maurice Quay, who called himself Agamemnon and dressed in clothes patterned after those on Greek vases, they let their hair and beards grow, slept at the foot of statues as if in communion with art, and, practicing what they believed to be pagan custom, bathed nude in the Seine. Other youths adopted a style of retirement from the world, the young men calling themselves *méditateurs* and the young women, *dormeuses.*[11]

A melancholic manner persisted during and after the Revolution, when channels for meaningful action became fewer. As Alfred de Musset wrote in his *Confession d'un enfant du siècle,* "Young people found a use for inactive strength in the affectation of despair. Scoffing at glory, religion, love, at everybody, is a great consolation for those who do not know what to do. . . . And it is easy to believe oneself wretched when one is only empty and bored."

A more strident and flamboyant tone also entered into the antics of extremists, reaching mass proportions by the mid-1830s. So fantastic were the posturings of many artists and would-be artists that they did violence to the poignant aspects of the plight of artists, and permitted or encouraged many people to view them as comic strip characters and to forget the real sufferings that motivated them.

Many of the aggressively pitched actions were defensive reactions, symptoms and rationalizations of the aimlessness artists felt in attaching themselves to an objectively useless activity without any certainty that diligence or ability would bring even minimal rewards. Even such a controlled though impassioned work as Shelley's *Defence of Poetry* was a symptom of the sense of rootlessness that engendered defensiveness. The defensive and aggressive actions of painters were stimulated by their new status in the social and artistic hierarchies. Some of the artist's hostility toward the bourgeois was a response to the stigma of being looked down upon as a manual worker, which persisted as a carry-over from the earlier social stratification.

Perhaps of greater importance, the ramifications of the idea of the autonomy of the artist had produced a dual image in which the artist regarded himself, and was regarded by others, both as a common man and as a superior being. The idea that every man can be an artist threatened the painter's sense of superiority, which requires something or someone to feel superior to, and led to a dramatization of differences by those aspirants who may have feared, secretly, that few existed. Most directly, the new situation of art encouraged exhibitionism as a means of attracting attention, since autonomy except for the great may result in a mortifying anonymity.

Many Bohemians trying to enact the new myth of the autonomous artist merely became minority group conformists. Youths searching for ideal images for themselves in physiognomy and in action found them in historical paraphernalia that seemed to affirm values from the past that were being lost. As future generations were to do with the trappings of cowboys, they flourished velvet capes and swords, imitating characters from the novels of Scott and Dumas. Artists like Eugène Devéria emulated Rubens with wide-brimmed hats which, moreover, cast mysterious "Spanish" and therefore passionate shadows over the eyes. If one's name was too "bourgeois," one could Anglicize, gothicize, or medievalize it. Auguste Maquet became Augustus Mac-Keat; other young Frenchmen became Lord Pilgrim, Fritz Karl, or Jehan. They also found more contemporaneous ideal images. In the frail, elegant young Delacroix, with his pale skin, well-trimmed moustache, thick black hair and alert black eyes, they saw a tempestuous temperament resembling Lord Byron; Achille Devéria, brother of Eugène, engraved their profiles together on the same medal.

The amorphous groups of artistically inclined youths who appropriated outstanding artists as their "leaders" were known as the *Jeunes-France*. This accent on youth may have been occasioned by the increasing numbers of their elders—through the extended life expectancy which had been a primary cause of the dramatic population growth of the previous hundred years.

> A whole generation of *Jeunes-France* wanted to have a "romantic" physiognomy, to appear *orageux,* to assume what they considered to be the stormy personality of Byron, Delacroix, or Berlioz by cultivating the appropriately mannered appearance: hair long and flowing or cut like a brush, pointed beard, beetling eyebrows, and lapels more "passionate" and flaring even than those of the dandies whose mannerisms became popular in France around the same time. Among the most ex-

treme postures were those of the *volcaniques*. According to a friend of one of these youths, "He cried, he yelled. . . . His habitual gesture is to press his chest with both hands in order to neutralize . . . the inner pressure of his heart which is formidable. Without this precaution, his thoracic cage . . . would be shattered by the pressure of the terrible organ, so much is it inflated, saturated with superhuman sentiments, with unheard of sensations, indeed overflowing with beautiful romantic things." [12]

A few artists and writers of the *Jeunes-France* formed the band of *Tartares* and then of the *Bouzingos* under the leadership of Petrus Borel, a painting student turned poet. They were evicted from a house Borel had rented when neighbors complained of their sitting in the garden nude in accordance with the teachings of the *Evadnistes,* a sect for the spiritual emancipation of women. In their next headquarters in the Rue d'Enfer, they caused a sensation by keeping a grinning skull over the mantelpiece in place of a clock, serving ice cream and custards in skulls, and dancing the *galop infernal* in the street.[13]

Not all the exhibitionists were associated with the arts. It was easy to confuse artists and *rapins* with political radicals in their common adoption of a melancholy or stormy mien. Mrs. Trollope, visiting from England where nothing like them was to be seen, was shocked by the "long and matted locks that hang in heavy, ominous dirtiness. . . . The throat is bare, at least from linen; but a plentiful and very disgusting profusion of hair supplies its place. . . . Some roll their eyes and knit their dark glances on the ground in fearful meditation; while others there be who, while gloomily leaning against a statue or a tree, throw such terrific meaning into their looks." [14]

The tempestuous and bizarre airs and antics of "romantic" youths in France created a vision of the artist which, as the delineation of a special type of personality or profession, did not have the same character across the Channel. In England there were individual nonconformists, such as Blake and Turner. Art and medical students were known for pranks and unconventional actions which were dismissed as a passing phase of youth. There was, however, no such mass movement as the *Jeunes-France*.

By belonging to a strong elite group, a French artist-demonstrator did not have to suffer as a lone, rejected deviant, for he had the support of what was virtually the special class to which he was considered to belong. Satisfactions derived from being part of an active group made it easier for him to bear hostility, amused tolerance, or intolerable indifference, and to assert the style of the Bohemian.

In England in the 1820s, artistic eccentricity was epitomized by the Ancients, a few young painters who clustered about Blake, then in his sixties, gathering in his house which they called "The House of the Interpreter." In continuation of the eighteenth-century vogue for the primitive, they wandered through Shoreham, their "Valley of Vision," to the watchwords of "Poetry and Sentiment," dreaming of the unsophisticated life in nature which they supposed had been led in earlier times. One of their number, Samuel Palmer, cultivated a semibald head and flowing beard and wore a cloak down to his heels in order to look "ancient." They called the children of John Linnell, another member of the group, "The Little Ancients." [15]

The principal embodiment of nonconformist behavior in England was the dandy, a symbol of protest within high society. The word "dandy" came to be used around 1813, at a time when dandyism seemed to fill a need in the refined, bored circle of the Regent. It invaded France with the wave of Anglomania in 1827, the same year Hugo's Preface to *Cromwell* created a sensation and Romantic paintings first appeared in great numbers in the Salon.

Although the new vogue was an English importation, the French had their own tradition of elegant affectation in the courtiers who had been the ornaments of Versailles. With nostalgia perhaps for times gone by, the French dandies seemed to seek distinction by approximating the elegances of their former aristocracy, as well as the English dandy-gentleman, as they strolled along the boulevards in their large cravats, bright vests, and coats of zephyr-blue, chestnut, or green among the black suits of the bourgeois. French dandyism of the 1830s and 1840s acquired the English verbal accoutrements of *sportsman, jockey, fashionable, lion, tiger.* It included also a repertoire of costume symbolic of political interests which was absent in England: Bonapartists in blue frock coats with large gold buttons, *ultras* in knee breeches, and liberals with gray hats.

In both countries, a more tempestuous taste modified the original restrained elegance which Beau Brummell had made fashionable. The simple, square lines and dominant silver tonality were succeeded by the more flamboyant, curvilinear ensemble which the Count d'Orsay popularized in the 1830s. In costumes shimmering with gold and jewels, coats thrown impetuously back over the shoulders to expose the sweep of waistcoat lapels, the dandies promenaded on the avenues of Paris and London, their scented, flowing hair a frame for curling lips and flashing eyes.[16]

These changes in silhouette were not limited to the costumes of dandies and Bohemians, but paralleled the shift in art from Neoclassic to Romantic and in the visual silhouette of everyday life. The classical columnar or willowy forms of women's dress that had prevailed during the Directory, Empire and Regency, in emulation of ancient Greek costume, became billowy or bulbous. Simplicity and lightness in furniture and decoration gave way to a greater complication, which became in turn the heaviness and clutter of the mid-century bourgeois and Victorian interior for which crowded eclectic paintings seemed an appropriate adornment.

Thus the eccentricities of dandies and Bohemians conformed in their broad outlines with tastes widespread among the public. With their disdainful stances and attempts to shock, they were not separating themselves from the rest of society but were reaching out to make themselves noticed as they protested, at opposite extremes, the dull center of moderation.

Of course, no one lived totally at any of the extremes of Bohemianism, dandyism, or moderation. Although the distortions of a stereotype make it seem a sort of social caricature, it does not, unlike true caricature, expose a person, but gives him the mask of a mass identity. The simplifications of stereotypes dull rather than sharpen observations. So effective were the posturings of the extremists that they succeeded in annexing to the old picture of the artist as a strange being the device of self-dramatization as an emblem of the integrity of the self, artistically and personally.

While the public chose the Bohemian as the prototype of the artist, and especially of the Romantic artist, most of the outstanding painters of the early nineteenth century were gentlemanly, or even dandies or bourgeois, in their general manners and conduct of life. One of the artists who was most advanced artistically appeared to be the most ordinary of men. Corot was a draper's apprentice until the age of twenty-six when his father gave him an allowance to enable him to dedicate his life entirely to painting. He seems to have been one of those rare individuals who actually achieves in his life that ideal of moderation and tranquillity which eludes most members of society. Tall and the picture of health, his ruddiness and the bourgeois cut of his clothes, his habit of gesticulating with the first object his hand met, were said to give him a certain ordinary appearance which contrasted with his innocent, "spiritual" conversation. His cheerfulness, kindliness, and love of a simple life earned him the title of "Papa Corot."

The greatest French Romantic painter was, in the eyes of Bohemian extremists, a deviate in terms of their professional class rather than in terms of polite society. Of high bourgeois origin and aristocratic sentiments, Delacroix was a polished gentleman and brilliant conversationalist whose fastidiousness of manner and dress led many to call him a dandy. Even in his youth Delacroix held aloof from the excesses of those who considered themselves Romantics. He viewed them with good humor, however, and wrote in their defense that "instead of being a species of savages outside of all human laws, some kind of adorers of formless fetishes, the Romantics or frantics, as you please, really have a kind of good sense permitting them to distinguish a certain ugliness from a certain beauty." The *Jeunes-France* thought his dress and demeanor, his careful keeping of accounts and hours, made him too bourgeois and "methodical"; they complained that he and Hugo were "as punctual as bureaucrats." [17]

Both Corot and Delacroix behaved pretty much according to the norms of the families into which they were born. Others sought to attain and accommodate themselves to the way of life of the gentleman or the bourgeois. So desperately did Ingres aspire to a conventional place in society that he broke off his engagement to the daughter of a famous Danish archaeologist because she was not decorous enough, marrying instead the proprietress of a dress shop.

Of course, the criteria of being a high bourgeois or a gentleman did not negate conflict; they simply required certain disguises. Haydon observed, "Lawrence and Sir George Beaumont [one of the most prominent English patrons, who was also a painter himself] are the two most perfect gentlemen I ever saw—both naturally irritable and waspish,

both controlling every feeling which is incompatible with good breeding." [18] Lawrence managed outwardly to control deep disturbances that
seemed at first sight to have no place on the polished surface of his
manners or of his art. While he cut a brilliant figure in the most elite
circles of London and the courts of the continent, friends were concerned about his anxiety, and his housekeeper pitied him as "Poor Sir
Thomas—always in trouble. Always something to worrit him." In later
years, canvases piled up which he seemed unable to drive himself to
finish. He went to extremes in preventing his inner disturbances from
violating the norms of good behavior. As head of the Royal Academy
after 1820, his disapproval of friction made him known as an advocate
of peace for peace's sake. With characteristic excessive politeness, he
apologized to the actress Eliza Farren for his "error in taste" in en-
titling her portrait simply *An Actress*.[19]

So well did Lawrence perfect his outward accommodation to the
gentleman's way of life, that his nervousness and small eccentricities
were passed over and even made him rather "interesting." But another
Royal Academician of low origin, Turner, never acquired the manners
or appearance of a gentleman.

The elegant Delacroix recalled that, on the single occasion they met,
in the early 1830s in Paris, "he made only a middling impression on me;
he had the look of an English farmer, black coat of a rather coarse type,
thick shoes." [20] Turner was indeed so insignificant in appearance that
Englishmen were in doubt that he could be a genius. Although he enjoyed the company of the elite and delighted in attending functions of
the Royal Academy, he seemed uncertain of how to conduct himself.
People complained of his "timidity" on one occasion, of his lack of
"respect to persons or circumstances" on another; of his taciturnity and of
his loquacity. His efforts to learn Greek, his labored poems and un-
grammatical speech and bad spelling, his mumbled and almost incom-
prehensible lectures as Professor of Perspective at the Royal Academy
made him seem somewhat clownish. He even deliberately offended what
was considered to be good form by establishing a large gallery in his
Harley Street house for the exhibition of his own work. At the same
time, he led a secretive and, according to rumor, a sexually scandalous
life.

Some contemporaries thought Turner's strong individuality would
have expressed itself less eccentrically in a milieu in which it did not

have to be defended so assiduously. "No one would have imagined, under his rather rough and cold exterior, how very strong were the affections which lay hidden beneath," said the daughter of a friend. "Oh! what a different man would Turner have been if all the good and kindly feelings of his great mind had been called into action; but they lay dormant, and were known to so very few." [21]

However, the "best" people tolerated Turner and even found him amusing, for he was an eccentric type with which the good society of England abounded. His frugality, seclusiveness, stubbornness, and outbursts of temper were actually like gentle caricatures of the self-reliance, aloofness, and independence which many an Englishman liked to cultivate in himself. He had not violated the social threshold of toleration in a society which nourished strange men even closer to its bosom in the persons of Beau Brummell and other dandies and rakes of the Regency and the court of George IV.

Besides, people expected an artist to be a bit odd: indeed, why else would one choose such an occupation? Englishmen and Frenchmen tolerated eccentric behavior much more from artists than from other persons. Part of the charm of these artists was that they were so extraordinary.

Eccentricity of an artist's life style did not mark him as cultivating any particular style of art. The oddities of David's former pupil Girodet, who died the year Romantic paintings began to shock Frenchmen, were as extreme as those of any Romantic "frantic." Oscillating between extremes of adaptation and withdrawal, he mixed much in society, elegantly dressed and perfumed. But he wore an old ragged outfit in his house where he allowed dust and spiderwebs to accumulate because he was afraid brooms were dangerous. So cautious was he that he would slowly open his studio door in order to look over his visitors before permitting them to enter. Friends said he would be overly respectful and polite, then suddenly impatient and irritable; in their eyes, he seemed to combine the arrogance of Michelangelo with the grace of Raphael. Girodet was said to be gentle, but he could be malicious. When he learned that a well-known actress was not satisfied with the portrait he had painted of her, he cut the picture into pieces and sent them to her in a box. To these destructive tokens he added public humiliation by exhibiting in the Louvre a painting of this lady as Danaë reclining nude in a shower of gold, with her lover as a turkey by her side.[22] Despite his eccentricities, this strange man was one of the most celebrated painters under Napoleon and Louis XVIII.

One of the most successful artists in England was also one of the most unconventional in behavior. Fuseli's manner fluctuated between diffident shyness and grand rages. Before coming to England, he had been even more exhibitionistic. After deserting the ministry in Switzerland and engaging in numerous escapades, he lived for a time in Rome where he mimicked the manners of Michelangelo. Later, in London, he became Keeper of the Royal Academy, and was cordially received in the company of aristocrats and other notables who admired his classical learning and witty conversation, punctuated with picturesque swearing followed by florid apologies.[23] Since he was a foreigner, his fiery aspect was not only tolerated but seemed to be expected in that insular world.

Even an extremely eccentric artist like William Blake could be a delightful adornment to a gathering of genteel ladies and gentlemen. They would put up with his crankiness when he complained, "The Enquiry in England is not whether a Man has Talents and Genius, but whether he is Passive and Polite and a Virtuous Ass." Defying this Enquiry, Blake delighted in shocking people. In a day when love of nature verged on pantheism, he declared, "Whoever believes in nature disbelieves in God, for nature is the work of the Devil." And he astonished a friend by declaring that he believed in polygamy, that he had committed many murders, that reason is the only sin, that careless, gay people are better than those who think.

Aside from an enthusiasm for the French Revolution, which many estimable Britons shared and later repented, Blake's everyday behavior was generally subdued and, in many respects, exemplary. A contemporary reported, "His observations, apart from his Visions and references to the spiritual world, were sensible and acute." His working habits were models for a respectable and modest shopkeeper in what Napoleon contemptuously referred to as a nation of shopkeepers. A steady worker, he died without leaving a debt. A visitor was willing to forgive the poverty in which he lived: "Nothing could exceed the squalid air both of the apartment and his dress, but in spite of the dirt—I might say filth—an air of gentility is diffused over him."[24]

Because Blake claimed that the muscular nudes and draped sibyls and prophets in his works came to him in visions, contemporaries and subsequent generations have not been able to decide whether he was insane or simply eccentric, a doubt in judgment which has long been entertained about visionaries, saints, and creative persons in general. Since psychosis is largely defined in social terms, the very genuineness of his hallucinations, combined with his unusual behavior, can be an argument for his mild insanity in terms of our culture. Even the fact that the symbols and forms he used were not as private as has often been supposed [25] does not rule out the possibility of mental disturbance, for even the art products of psychotics in a clinical setting have identifiable cultural features. Insistence on his complete sanity may be a symptom of the newer aspect of the myth of the artist as an eminently healthy person. The possibility that Blake suffered from a mild psychosis does not, of course, reflect on his fine accomplishments as poet and artist. During his lifetime, even those who considered him insane could stand in respect and awe of his "divine madness," long thought to be an ingredient of genius.

    In not fitting the image of the mad or odd artist at all, an incontestably sane and solid man like John Constable irritated people with his independent behavior. Since there seemed to be no ready explanation for his nonconformity, it threatened all the more the shibboleths of everyday life.

His very naturalness of manner got him in trouble with elements of society demanding artificiality or stylized naturalness. He disdained Brighton as "the receptacle of the fashion and offscouring of London," with its conceits of dress, manners, and conversation. What seemed his honesty and ruggedness, "frank outspeakingness and fearlessness" to some, appeared "coarse habits" and "great vanity and conceit" to others. A contemporary said that his manner, "sometimes savouring of rusticity and destitute of the artifice and convention of society . . . subjected him and his peculiarities, however, to assailments from anonymous, unjudicious, and pointless criticism, which a less genuine and more courtly carriage might have saved him from, or transformed into praise or fame, patronage or profit." [26] Those who objected to Constable's "peculiarities" could also see them reflected in his radical art style.

On the other hand, contemporaries saw a sharp contrast between

Delacroix's artistic practice and his elegance of manner and speech. In the fashionable salons he frequented, people would say, "What a shame such a charming man should paint like that." [27] Like Carlyle, they expected the artist's personality to be revealed in his work. But the artist conceals as much as he reveals in his painting, whether deliberately or inadvertently. An art style may be a compensation for, rather than a reflection of, the artist's "nature."

Both driving and restraining Delacroix, in his life and in his art, was a system of controls, operating partially in the interests of disguising the weaknesses of this man who seemed so assured in society and bold in his art. At the beginning of his career, Delacroix wrote about the nature of what he called his "defense." "How weak I am, how vulnerable and open to surprise on all sides. . . . Haven't people often taken me for a man of firm will? The mask is everything." As an ordering influence and a way of establishing a guide and model for himself, he began a regimen of constant activity and self-examination which he kept up all his life. He started his *Journal* as "a way of calming the emotions that have troubled me for so long." The year before he painted *The Massacre of Chios,* he determined, "Habitual orderliness of ideas is your sole road to happiness, and to reach it, orderliness in all else, even the most casual things, is needed." [28]

A constructive outcome of this ordering was a creative use of his deficiencies. For instance, his style of drawing was not merely the expression of a "natural" spontaneity, but resulted from working hard at an element in which he felt weak. Delacroix's strong controls had a constrictive as well as a creative effect on his art. The too obvious composing of many of his more ambitious works seems a frame for the more passionate color and brushwork. This inhibition had been present in the artist as a young man. Already in 1822, Gros had referred to Delacroix's art as "Rubens chastened." Because of his eloquence in speech and writing, the discrepancy between his artistic ideals and their realization is especially striking. Although he believed geniuses benefit from a loosening of the grip of reason while at work, he was wary about the dangers of obscurity and formlessness. Delacroix's inability to attain in his major paintings, as distinct from his drawings, his ideal of spontaneous creation, was actually consistent with his double ideal of a strongly controlled and passionate expressiveness, resulting from the imposition of order on what he felt to be a disorderly disposition.

As large numbers of "Romantics or frantics" pretended to adopt the Romantic style in art with the facility with which they put on a Rubenesque hat, the great painter became disgusted with them. The flamboyance of even an outstanding painter, or writer like Dumas, was antipathetic to Delacroix, who said, "I can't stand it when the artist exhibits himself." [29]

Delacroix's attitude harmonized with a view of the creative individual as a person in whom the center of the self is not confined in the ego, a view which coexisted with the belief that the artist is endowed with a "peculiar nature." Echoing eighteenth-century thought which regarded personality as almost an abstract universal, Keats wrote that the true poet "has no character . . . no identity," but becomes "annihilated" in the character of those about him and concerns himself with revealing their essential natures. Delacroix believed that "the way to be expressive . . . to express oneself, in a word," is to be "in harmony with the turn of mind peculiar to the men of the time." Admiring Rubens and Rembrandt, he noted, "Mediocre men cannot have such daring; they never get outside themselves." [30]

As excesses of originality and individuality led to a stereotyping of both Romantic art and conduct in their terms, artists themselves reacted against principles that had seemed more attractive when desired than when practiced. With disdain for that very individuality and freedom which had been so much sought in all areas of life, including the arts, and with a nostalgia for community identity, Baudelaire wrote of the Salon of 1846:

. . . *The present state of painting is the result of an anarchic freedom which glorifies the individual, however feeble he may be, to the detriment of communities—that is to say, of schools [which] are nothing else but organizations of inventive force.*

This glorification of the individual has necessitated the infinite division of the territory of art. The absolute and divergent liberty of each man, the division of effort and the disjunction of the human will have led to this weakness, this doubt and this poverty of invention. A few sublime and long-suffering eccentrics are a poor compensation for this swarming chaos of mediocrity. Individuality—that little place of one's own—has devoured collective originality. . . . It is the painter that has killed the art of painting. [31]

When there was such ambivalence within the artistic community about the character of art and of the artist, it is not surprising to find it also among the general public. The creation by artists of their own elite, which had been instigated by their changed relationships with the public, resulted in a combined admiration and envy on the part of the public. In a way, the ordinary man had a closer sense of identification with the artist than formerly, stemming from the high regard for the autonomous individual which the Enlightenment had nurtured. The artist typified the ideal of the autonomous person more strongly even than the successful businessman. He took chances without the assurance that hard work would enable him to achieve, as did followers of established occupations, even the moderate success that would bring a certain amount of respect from his fellows. The artist, by affirming in his work those ideals of freedom and individuality which were largely catchwords and slogans in society, sowed the seeds of guilt and envy in those who did not pursue their psychological cultural goals as consistently.

For if there was discontent on the part of many artists *with* the middle classes, there was also discontent *within* the middle class, intensified by its suppression of its own ideals. Artists were only one of a number of other discontented elites—including the old aristocrats and the new bureaucratic and professional groups—which the recently powerful middle class, itself a discontented economic elite before the Revolution, created or perpetuated. Such uneasy groups and persons are never trivial footnotes to the times but are symptomatic of more widespread feelings of social estrangement.

The bourgeois also experienced social frustrations which, as with artists, often burst into one form or another of deviant behavior. There were even perfectly respectable social occasions in which the average man behaved differently than in his ordinary life. At the masquerades, street carnivals, and the theaters of the boulevards, in the frenzies of the galop and the waltz, the citizen of Paris could assume a role more intense and exuberant than his routine identity as shopkeeper or government clerk. But few except artists had the opportunity to express such passionateness or to loosen repressions in their daily lives and work.

When a belief existed that anyone *could* be an artist, the layman often, at least secretly, wished more than ever to exercise what had once been considered the artist's prerogatives. In choosing his passionate, rebellious aspect as their image of the artist, the public as well as many artists revealed a picture of the kind of life they wanted to lead, the kind of men they wanted to be in fantasy. The stereotype permitted them to ridicule what they could not or would not be in reality. The picture of the disdained and admired culture hero, the artist, was therefore a projection of more general uncertainties about the character and place in the world of Everyman, who was forced by the liberating expectations aroused by the Enlightenment to be his own protagonist or, betraying these expectations, to submit to a Hero.

Attitudes and aspirations that entered into the new symbolic relationship of public and artist also affected the course of development of themes concerned with such basic elements of life as love and death, and with the orientation and acts of men, ordinary and extraordinary.

SIX

Metamorphoses of the Hero

While the artist became a new kind of culture hero, the hero as a principal theme vanished from painting as an image of man. The process of dethronement of the hero from the dominating position in art he had occupied since antiquity was gradual. And it was intimately related to the artist's problem in finding imagery meaningful to the people of his time.

Painters had to decide not only what kind of characters and actions to portray, but also where in space and time the scene should be laid. In antiquity artists had depicted celebrities, particularly athletes and military heroes who were close to the observer's immediate experience, and this practice was partially revived in sculpture in the fifteenth century. But during the Middle Ages and the Renaissance it was customary for painters to place gods and devils, priests, kings and knights in some imaginary setting or to show personages who had been dead for centuries in contemporary dress and locales. Authenticity of detail or historical accuracy did not matter when the picture was considered to be true because of the generally accepted universal truth of its content. In the strongly stratified societies of the past, the greatness of these heroic or superhuman figures was not usually questioned.

As a greater sense of history developed, it revealed the relative value of epochs of time and of human worth, and instilled a confidence in progress. The idea of progress gradually developed into a belief in the perfectibility of man.[1] As high strata in the social hierarchy became more widely attainable, the old images of types that seemed great by virtue of their remoteness in time or social accessibility were undermined. With the shift of belief from a fixed supernatural sphere to a secular world involved in the flux of history, the stability and standards of greatness—in themes and characters as well as in the techniques of the work of art—became increasingly problematic. In the seventeenth century, the conventional hero or gentleman was satirized, not only in picaresque literature but also in paintings where gypsies or other clever scoundrels made him look foolish by outwitting him. Caravaggio and Georges de La Tour painted the Holy Family and saints as humble folk, while the Dutch specialized in burghers or peasants for themselves alone.

Awareness of the relativity of time and of human worth also led to a sharper distinction in art between time and people as imagined and as experienced, and to a new stress on real experience. It had been the custom to glorify contemporary heroes with allegorical trappings. But in the sixteenth and seventeenth centuries artists also painted a class of picture in which they rendered a fairly recent event, usually a battle or its aftermath, devoid of allegory as if the spectator were present: thus in *The Surrender of Breda* Velásquez presented the military commanders as ordinary mortals ungarlanded by angels.

In the Enlightenment, special problems arose for the types and roles of figures in painting, as in the world. With the new outlook on the world as a system in which man—no matter how strong willed, heroic, or endowed with genius—no longer occupied a pseudo or semidivine place, it became necessary either to eliminate or to renovate the heroic. Painters created new images as carriers of grandeur and heroism by blending the traditional Platonic idea of the desirability of using the actions of gods and heroes as themes for art with the newer ideas about the nature of human beings which enveloped all classes.

A nonheroic or anti-heroic art intervened between the grand Baroque and its revival. Although in life the hope of improving one's lot in the world intensified the sense of the past as being past, the bourgeois making his way in the world, together with the aristocrat who remained attached to the old ways of life, did not necessarily desire, in art, to focus his attention on the everyday world. He would let his imagination play, not only on the past, but also on the spatially remote realm of the exotic. Fashionable ladies liked to have their portraits painted in oriental costume to symbolize, though quite artificially, the "primitive" as related to the "natural." With the people in Watteau's paintings, the bourgeois as well as the aristocrat could inhabit a make-believe world of the present, the timeless existence of reverie, a waking dream, which affords a sampling opportunity, like play, for the imagination. The hero was lost in the sunny gardens of English conversation pieces and in the little amorous conquests of the *fêtes galantes* with their capricious masked courtiers through whom life could be envisaged as a flirtatious game.

Many artists longed to paint more heroic themes of the sort that had traditionally been set forth in historical painting, by which was usually meant stories from the Bible or the ancient world. This type of painting embodied the loftiness and sublimity of the virtuous deeds of the hero. It was associated, moreover, with the prestige of the great artists of the past. However, what constituted the heroic was no longer clear. Voltaire, like Hume and Gibbon, tried to ridicule and destroy the exaggerated pretensions of heroes, saints, and other immortal beings, though at the same time, he wanted to raise history above the "all-too-human," the accidental and merely personal.

These conflicting desires were reconciled in art by the infiltration of mere mortals, endowed with human feelings, virtues and vices, into the superhuman framework of the history piece. While the Rococo and the English conversation piece eliminated the epic hero, in historical painting the ordinary mortal stepped from his artistic province of the genre picture to invade the realm of the great and sacred. In striving to become a being who can partake of the marvellous, he eventually made of the hero a mere protagonist.

Although different conditions of patronage had created a smaller market for heroic paintings in England, they also suffered a decline in France as Louis XIV's court went bankrupt and many courtiers themselves grew tired of bravura. Around the middle of the eighteenth century, these paintings revived in considerable numbers under the stimulus of state patronage. Inspired by the ideas of the English and French philosophers, the royal officials who conceived and directed the program wished to inculcate knowledge and virtue throughout society—not to confine art to a small coterie of the nobility, but to make the examples illustrated in didactic art visible to the common people through ambitious schemes for museums and exhibitions. They hoped to transmit worthy ideas and sentiments through a revival of the seventeenth-century grand manner rather than through stimulation of new styles or subjects.

It was the official French position that one of the objects of painting was to transmit great examples of heroism.[2] Partially a patriotic reaction to the colonial wars, this position was also strengthened by the discoveries and excavations at Herculaneum and Pompeii. For about forty years before the political Revolution, commissions encouraged painters to render pictorial tableaux evoking the ancient classical world and modern patriotism, such as Vien's *Hector urging his brother Paris to take arms for the defense of his country*. Whether or not all the artists who painted such pictures were actually imbued with patriotic and heroic sentiments, the material rewards were hard to resist at a time when painting had become so precariously related to the world in which the artist lived.

The ancient themes with their old attachments and human relationships were not always satisfying. Even in the first quarter of the century, artists considered alternative ways to represent virtue in accord with the feeling for the immediacy of real experience that made genre art so widely appreciated. Hogarth showed that morality could be preached through ordinary persons, even rakes and harlots, as well as through saints and stock heroes. But though some artists tried to depict grandeur or heroism in terms of recent events in their real settings, they rarely dropped the support of allegory. Not until fifty years later did a new type of historical painting, aiming at accuracy of fact and costume, become fashionable in France.

The new type was anticipated in England in 1771 by the American painter Benjamin West with his *Death of General Wolfe*. In this large canvas, West referred to an event of 1759 without allegory, saying, "The same truth which gives law to the historian should govern the painter." Although, as military archaeologists have shown, West's treatment was not completely true to the facts, his use of contemporary costume gave the spectator the feeling of being present at the event, if not actually participating in it. At the same time, by locating the scene in the exotic setting of America, not with cherubs but a real Red Indian, a veritable noble savage, looking on, West preserved a sense of the remote and the marvellous which was believed essential for instilling reverence for the hero. There was a greater threat to veneration in Copley's *Death of Chatham*. Here the artist approximated reportage by having all who had been present at the minister's death in Parliament sit for their portraits, which he included in the picture; thus he brought the spectators of 1783 into direct contact with an event that had occurred only five years earlier on their home ground.[3]

Forward-looking as they were, these paintings were also compatible with academic theory. While a mere mortal ascends the pedestal formerly occupied by mythological or classical figures, he is further imbued with pathos and the aura of the superhuman by the setting of his death scene in the general design of the *pietà* theme of traditional Christian iconography.

It seems appropriate that the revolution of real experience in monumental history painting of the eighteenth century was effected by West and Copley, painters from the land that was the first to proclaim officially the *Novus Ordo Seclorum*. Perhaps these artists from the new world, finding it harder to believe in heroes that could not be depicted as mortals, also found it credible that mere humans could become heroes, as happened so often on the expanding frontier. It seems appropriate also that this type of picture should have been commissioned in England, where social mobility accelerated a greater political implementation than on the continent of the Enlightenment's belief in the rights and dignity of all men.

Historical painting in England also represented an attempt by connoisseurs, enraptured by the art seen on their European travels, to impose it on a society where there was no market for it except in the popular medium of prints—a situation which had led Hogarth to invent the small moral history piece as a substitute for the great histories he longed to paint. Thus metamorphoses of the hero in painting were not merely reflections of the social metamorphoses of real life, though they would not have occurred in the same way without the changes in society.

Around the same time, in the equivocally reformist atmosphere during the monarchy of Louis XVI, a greater feeling for the immediacy of real experience entered the official art of France. For instance, in 1769 Vien painted *The Inauguration of the Equestrian Statue of the King* without angels descending from heaven to herald the event, as had been customary practice.[4] For the most part, however, in this country where history painting was ensconced in tradition, the new rage for authenticity of costume and décor was concentrated on the past, combining reality and remoteness.

Through their own traditionally classical education and a fad for classical décor and fashion stirred up by the archaeological discoveries, people understood and appreciated David's painstaking study of the detail of Roman costume in *Brutus* and the literary and ideological references of his *Horatii*. Whether imitating David's art, as Delécluze reported, or influenced by Rousseauistic ideas of naturalness, people soon stopped powdering their hair and wearing corsets and talon shoes; dress became simpler and lighter, furniture and architecture more severe, and etiquette less elaborate.[5]

The vogue for historical authenticity extended also to subjects dealing with national history. However, the attempt at accuracy in medieval and Renaissance décor and costume was in direct conflict with the academic prohibition against modern (which meant nonclassical) dress for the noble figures of art. In contrast with the formalized rendering of classical subjects, the new interest in authenticity also involved greater attempts at realism through variations in the expressions and appearance of historical personages, extending even to hair and beard styles and the carriage of their heads. Particularly from 1777 to 1785, the life of Henry IV was one of the favorite themes, as it was to be for Romantic painters.[6]

Whether because of an anti-historical attitude fostered by a faith in the present that infused economic and social life or a trans-historical feeling in tune with a widespread vogue for the occult in all classes of society,[7] some artists rejected the veracious or semi-veracious history picture and cultivated the fantastic style of "spiritual portraiture." James Barry, whom Blake considered the greatest artist of the eighteenth century, used it as an antidote to the historicism of West. It carried over into styles as different as the spiritualized sculpture of Flaxman and the dreamlike paintings of Girodet. The revival of interest in Shakespeare afforded opportunity to combine history and fantasy—an interest epitomized by the opening in 1789 of Alderman John Boydell's gallery, a collection of 167 paintings by Romney, West, Opie, Fuseli, Reynolds and others, done on commission to illustrate the works of the Bard.

Choice of the historical or fantastic type of art depended on the individual artist's psychological disposition as well as on his commission. Speaking of the difficulty of painting scenes from Homer, who had become a favorite with painters and writers, David confessed, "As for myself, I thought to show more prudence than they, in adopting an historical event of which I should remain the master and which I would poeticize in my own way, or in spite of all my efforts, I would always seem inferior and prosaic. . . . I do not like or feel the Marvellous; I cannot be easy except with the help of a real event." [8]

In depicting real events, past or present, French artists created works that served a social and even a political purpose. With emphasis on the creative impulse as purpose rather than pleasure, David wished to put a concept of art inherited from his predecessors at the service of the Revolution. "The arts should contribute strongly to public education," he told the Convention. "It is thus that characteristics of heroism and civic virtue, offered for the inspection of the people, will electrify their soul and nurture in it the passions of glory and devotion to their country." [9]

Although David recorded a contemporary event directly in *The Tennis Court Oath,* there was in general a preference for metaphorical allusions to the present in terms of the past. The frame of reference was the same in painting as in intellectual and public life—the culture of the ancient world which had impelled the government of Louis XV to commission a series of busts of ancient heroes like Coriolanus, Spartacus, and Leonidas as part of a project for an open air sculpture museum,[10] and which provided the incubating ideological atmosphere in which Danton, Robespierre, Marat, and other leaders of the Revolution were born. Ironically, while the aesthetic reformism of the aristocrats led to the cherished *révolution frappante* of Vien, their analogous social reformism made them the unwitting precursors of the political revolutionaries of 1789.

The fact that David's themes corresponded with the symbolic frame of reference of the leaders of the Revolution led them to select his painting as their official art, rather than the subjects of such contemporaries as Vincent and Ménageot which evoked the old monarchy. Festooning the Revolution with motifs that had been in general use in decoration and architecture under the old regime, David designed costumes and settings for the festivals with which the new leaders hoped to inculcate stoical virtues, in emulation of ancient Sparta's pageants for mass education which Rousseau had believed could be used in the modern state.[11]

Stock themes were often invested with contemporary social and politi-

cal meanings. Democratic sentiments, which contemporaries had recognized to exist in such pictures as the *Death of Wolfe* and *Brutus,* became more explicit. People interpreted *The Rape of the Sabine Women,*
which David conceived and designed about 1790, as symbolic of the need
for reconciliation after the Terror. David's pupils continued to use this
kind of symbolism. In *Marcus Sextus returning from exile finding his
wife dead,* painted by Guérin who was to become the teacher of Géricault, Delacroix, Delaroche and Scheffer, people saw more than an
illustration of ancient history; they saw the plight of the émigrés who
were returning from exile in 1799.[12]

In the early years of the nineteenth century, there was a continuing
taste for great ancients in France and also in England, where the exhibition in 1817 of *The Judgment of Brutus* by the French history
painter Thière attracted so many visitors that there was hardly standing room in the gallery.[13]

The frame of reference was often intensely personal. In great men of
the distant past artists and others found figures with whom they felt an
affinity, a second already great self in which they could see recognized
and realized their ideas of grandeur and of achievements or actions
denied them. Self-identification was not always unconscious. In heroes
of Roman history, Haydon found active and intrepid images, such as
Curtius Leaping into the Gulf and *Dentatus;* frustrated and harassed
in real life, he chose to paint the moment when Dentatus "was just
rushing out to cut his way through his host of assailants." [14] Ingres,
keeping out of the area of conflict and possible disappointment by his long
residence in Rome, was attracted to ancient heroes who were more removed from the cares of life, like the God Jupiter or a lyrical genius
surrounded by other artists and scholars in the *Apotheosis of Homer.*

Classical figures and designs did not, however, monopolize the field,
even at the height of the Revolution. Revolutionary festivals were
adorned with the masonic and illuminist trappings of pyramids and obe-
lisks as well as with classical arches and columns—all part of the wave
of religious millenarism and exultant humanitarianism that swept over
thousands of people in the latter part of the eighteenth century and
found in the great Revolution a possible medium of universal regeneration that was only incidentally political. As the integrity of the Revolution became compromised, the more austere images of Neoclassicism appeared less convincing. Perhaps as much for this reason as in pursuit of

the idea of the purity of earlier stages of civilization, David turned from the Romans to the Greeks and then softened his style somewhat more to meet the tastes of Napoleon, leading some of his own pupils to attack him as a reactionary, as a "Vanloo."

Napoleon's desire to give his regime a semblance of legitimacy, by cloaking it with imagery connected with the past, encouraged a more varied system of references—medieval and Rococo as well as Greek, Roman, and Egyptian (which enjoyed a revival with the North African campaigns). The Emperor reached out to spiritual ancestors through his triumphal arches. But he rejected David's designs à la grecque for the uniforms of state officials, preferring instead the three-cornered hat, sword, breeches, and buckle shoes of the old regime. Reminiscent of themes popular before the Revolution was a vogue for medieval subjects and events made newly popular by the novels of Sir Walter Scott and the spread of "Gothic" tastes in France. Napoleon wished to be identified with heroes from various times and places: in David's fiery equestrian portrait of *Bonaparte Crossing the St. Bernard Pass* (1801), the names of heroes of antiquity and the Middle Ages are marked on the rocks in the foreground. Napoleon also honored Girodet for placing him and his generals among the immortals in his painting of the pseudo-medieval poem *Ossian,* and he commissioned Ingres to do a painting of Ossian for his bedroom. "Within ten years the study of the antique will be abandoned," David prophesied on visiting the Salon of 1808. "Also, all these gods, these heroes will be replaced by knights, troubadours singing beneath the windows of their ladies, at the foot of an old turret." [15]

More immediately, they were displaced by the image of the man who had himself proclaimed Emperor. In an embattled Europe where Everyman was "privileged" to serve in the conscripted armed forces that replaced the old mercenary dynastic armies, the stoic Roman virtues of the late eighteenth century were accommodated to the requirements of the adventurous, aggressive man of action who led them. While leaders of the Revolution had sought to give institutional body to their ideals, Napoleon himself became their embodiment. David apostrophized him in terms of the sanctity of ancient art: "Oh! my friends, what a beautiful head he has! It is pure, it is grand, it is as beautiful as the antique. . . . He is such a man as altars would have been raised to in antiquity; yes, my friends; yes, my dear friends! Bonaparte is my hero!" [16] Napoleon's powers of attraction were extra-national in scope, luring even the enemy.

As early as 1801, there was a popular exhibition in London of portraits of Napoleon, during the same year that Beechey showed a full-length study of his adversary, Lord Nelson. Beechey's work was condemned for not being heroic enough, "more like a caricature than a portrait of the Hero of the Nile." [17]

The grand pose for heroes was so widely expected that Turner was criticized for not painting the soldiers in *Hannibal Crossing the Alps* in sufficiently heroic attitudes. Goethe, while admiring Flaxman's illustrations of Dante for their lively invention, naïveté, naturalism, and power of composition, regretted that they were weak in the heroic motif.[18]

With the shifting of roles in social life, changes came about also in the stances and relationships of figures in art. Even earlier in the eighteenth century, the actions of human beings in art had become so ambiguous that in many Rococo paintings the statues seem to be more alive than the people. In the imagined repertoire of greatness are the stiff postures and haughty stares of the statuesque Roman heroes of David, like actors in the plays which inspired many of the paintings.[19] But expressions stormily animated by flashing glances and flowing hair, which had appeared before the Revolution, characterize Napoleon and his generals, and then the figures in Romantic art. They are reminiscent of the gestures of ideal and deviant types in the life of the times.

The relation of the individual to the group was profoundly altered in art, as well as in the world. David's stoic Horatii and Leonidas were tied in definite pictorial ways to other figures whom they seemed to dominate by will as well as by physical prowess. Each of the characters in the eighteenth-century tableaux had a well defined role to play in a precisely delineated and circumscribed drama. Later, in the battle pieces of the Empire, the individual is a participant in a big spectacle. He is lost in it or at its mercy. In many of these canvases, action is dispersed and not concentrated in single heroic figures or in small groups. Complementing the heroic, composed figure of the leader, the *mass* of the army is heroic, though with an adulterated heroism. For the army is an impersonal juggernaut, bringing to grim fruition an eighteenth-century no-

The Louvre, Paris. Archives photographiques

Gros, *Napoleon on the Battlefield of Eylau* (detail), 1808

tion of man as a machine, thus negating the essential willfulness of the hero. These paintings also seem to affirm that mass sentiment, at once self-conscious and impersonal, known as nationalism. Patriotic sentiments were superseded as the state came to be considered in respect of the ruled rather than the ruler—a shift in the frame of reference of despotism epitomized by the change of identification from the Sun King who is said to have declared, *"L'état, c'est moi,"* to the Corsican commoner who had himself proclaimed Emperor of the French.[20] But in general, not until later in the nineteenth century was the leader lost in the mass action of French battle paintings.

It is hard to imagine Napoleon permitting himself to be absent from his victory pictures. Wilkie's painting of the victory at Waterloo, which was commissioned by Wellington himself, featured a closely packed mass of Chelsea pensioners discussing and celebrating the glad tidings, removed from the scene and the hero. This was due only in part to English understatement and self-effacement. For despite the efforts of such painters as Hamilton and West, the heroic motif was still not firmly established in English art. A critic described a big exhibition held at the Royal Academy during the Hundred Days as "Great in trifles—in portrait, in landscape, in fancy and poetical compositions—but deficient in History, in the Grand, and in the Sublime." [21] Haydon was therefore justified in his many complaints that the heroic style of history painting was not encouraged in England. At least, his intense efforts in its behalf cast a beam of greatness on himself, the heroic failure.

In France, where, after the fall of Napoleon, historical painting continued to have strong supports in the strength of tradition and official patronage, a young generation carried still farther the process West had set in motion half a century earlier. Some of the older artists also had executed paintings which appeared to have been based on first-hand observation. These paintings rivaled other types in prestige. Delacroix marveled that Gros, in *Louis XVIII fleeing the Tuileries the night of March 20, 1815,* had elevated "the modern subject to the ideal." [22]

On the other hand, Géricault did not try to dignify the canvas by including a figure of high rank in his *Raft of the Medusa.* More than a century before the newsreel, he contrived to give the spectator a vivid vicarious experience of the anguish of the survivors of a momentous shipwreck. In a sort of frozen motion Cinemascope, he carefully constructed this monstrously large visual dramatization of the disaster from newspaper reports and the accounts of survivors. Like many painters of the Empire, Géricault located the quality of heroism not primarily in an individual—not even in the dominant one—but in the group, which thrusts in an epic triangle toward the horizon where the rescue ship appears. In paintings of individual soldiers, isolated from the scene of

The Louvre, Paris. Archives photographiques

Géricault, *The Raft of the Medusa*, 1819

battle, Géricault had already focused on the anonymous common man.
While formerly the dominant figure of a monumental group would have
been at least a soldier, if not the monarch, in the *Medusa* Géricault
made him a Negro underling. This was not an innovation, but a continuation from the eighteenth century of a type of picture in which a
Negro was often shown as a member of the crew, in order to point up
the humanitarian agitation of the time. Géricault himself painted portraits of Negroes and sketched the misery of the slave market. In
the *Medusa,* by making a mere man of the superman, by replacing the
monarch or his soldiers with a group of victims who suffered as the
result of the governmental negligence supposed to have been responsible
for the shipwreck, Géricault seemed to proclaim that the role of hero
could be played by any man, even an outcast.

Actually, for a long time some of the principal figures in world
of art had been outcasts. During the Middle Ages, virtuous saints competed in popularity with that angel cast out of heaven, Satan, the
supreme antihero. Bandits and rapists spice the art of the seventeenth
century. In public life as well, some of the favorite heroes of all time
including Alexander, Caesar and Napoleon, were criminals in their
depredations against whole peoples. With roots in his old identity as
sorcerer or magician or rebel that lie deep in the mythological matrix,
the artist himself partakes of the double nature of the hero. The
legendary being acquired a criminal aspect from the forbidden nature of
his activity which, as with Daedalus and Prometheus, conflicted with
the power of the demiurge, and from his identity as the possessor of
magical power who made a pact with Satan.[23] In such a picture as
Blake's *Satan Smiting Job with Boils,* the artist might imagine himself as
embodied by the villain or the victim.

The new autonomy of the artist and the greater viability of the aspirations of the common man gave special potency to images of the
legendary artist and of other heroes and antiheroes who, as exceptional
beings, were considered exempt from ordinary rules. The lawless aspect

The Metropolitan Museum of Art, New York. Gift of Edward Bement, 1917

Blake, *Satan Smiting Job with Boils* (detail from engraving from the Book of Job), 1821-26

of the antihero seems an appropriate accompaniment for the new terms of social dominance whereby great numbers of men were able, though low-born, to assert themselves through their own initiative which, while socially acceptable, was often lawless. Climaxing and assailing the eighteenth-century idea of man living in harmony with natural law, man seemed to consider himself exempt from all outer laws.

Particularly in the 1820s and 1830s when no vigorous or inspiring leaders appeared in public life, many people found them in antiheroes who defy social conventions. There was a widespread taste in visual art and literature for portrayals of Satan and of analogs for Satan, such

as Faust. The devil was a popular fellow, though not the seriously re
garded personage he had been in the Middle Ages, and several *foyers d*
satanisme came into being. Delécluze complained, after listening to *De*
Freischütz which inaugurated Romantic opera, that a fascination wit
Satan "dominates taste at present, as shepherds in pink breeches . .
were the rage for forty years. Which is the more ridiculous?" [24]

Criminal types in general were in such vogue in the arts that the
appeared in various contexts. Heine wrote sarcastically of *Liberty Lead*
ing the People that Delacroix's "hero who storms around the galleys i
his features has certainly the smell of the criminal court in his abominabl
garments." [25] And the same year in England, Bulwer demonstrated i
his novel *Paul Clifford* that criminals can be dandies and dandies
criminals. Indeed, the social deviancy of criminal types corresponded t
those other manifestations of protest, dandyism and bohemianism, whicl
also regarded conventional society in negative terms.

Some flamboyant artists tried to affect the image of historical o
literary antiheroes, such as those of "Monk" Lewis, Mrs. Shelley, an
Byron. "I had put on, along with others, a mask," Dumas recalled. "I
1832 I felt myself a Manfred, a Childe Harold." The image was carrie
into the urgencies of the contemporary world. As if distorting th
eighteenth-century idea of man living in harmony with himself, a Frencl
student demanded, "When will French youths learn that the man o
modern times is a law unto himself?" [26]

In general, artists, and the public as well, still desired heroe
from the bright realm of noble ideals and lofty sentiments rather thar
the dark abodes of the antihero. Romantics, like the artists who precede
them, were nurtured on, and deeply affected by, the culture of th
ancient world. Stendhal had written in his autobiography, *The Life o*
Henry Brulard, of himself as a youth, "I was full of the heroes of Roma
history; I looked upon myself as a future Camillus or Cincinnatus, o
a mysterious mixture of the two. . . . I never tired of studying th

features of . . . famous men whose lives I should have liked to imitate.
. . I thought of nothing but honour and heroism." But unlike Stendhal
and other youths of the last decades of the eighteenth century whose
earlier hopes were dashed in maturity, young men of the Restoration began life by seeking other contexts of identification.

By the time the Romantic movement had coalesced in the 1820s, the
new generation regarded the culture of the ancient world, in so far as it
had become a formula for the arts, as inappropriate. The liberal and
anticlerical paper *Le Globe* insisted in 1825, "The world is still full
of men who have the simplicity of believing that one can satisfy the
needs of the nineteenth century with the books of antiquity as if, above
all, it were not necessary to be of one's country and of one's time. No,
no, it is not with the language of Athens and Rome that one can speak
to the moderns." [27]

It was in modern Greece, struggling for liberty against the Turks,
that many young men found an image with which they could identify
their own desires for freedom in life. Like Byron, they went to Greece
in search of employment for their heroic impulses. Mendouze, an ex-
pupil of David who had given up painting to study Greek, was killed on
the island of Chios. [28] Other artists who stayed at home followed the
wars closely and depicted them in their works, the most celebrated of
which is Delacroix's *Massacre of Chios*.

Nevertheless, despite their frequent use of the refrain *il faut être de
son temps,* Romantics as well as Neoclassicists continued to express the
concerns of their time largely in terms of past time. They turned to a
different past, however, and sought identification with it or allusion to
their own times through medieval and Renaissance themes. In fulfilling
David's prophecy of a prevalence of knights and troubadours, they prepared the ground for future exaggerated accusations of escapism.

Exploitation of historical themes was not necessarily a cue to the
artist's own sentiments or attachments. Certain themes and styles were
still largely ways to money and fame, as they had been, quite respectably,
for even the most advanced artists for centuries. Since the upstart Napoleon had wished to give his regime a semblance of legitimacy through
imagery connected with French monarchs of the past, it is not surprising
that the restored Bourbons wished to remind the public of their heredi-

tary claims to the throne. Like Louis XVI, they commissioned painting
dealing with the history of France, and particularly with the reign of
Henry IV, the first Bourbon king. These historical subjects were painted
not only by such artists as Ingres and Gérard, whose studio had been a
sort of manufactory under the Empire, but also by young Romantics, in
cluding Eugène Delacroix.

As the political situation began to deteriorate in the last years of the
Restoration, Frenchmen—artists and nonartists—cultivated wholly non
national terms of reference. Things English, in particular, symbolized
liberal values. The new rage resembled another wave of Anglomania be
fore the Revolution of 1789, when the French had aped English clubs
horseracing, and even toyed with English political ideas. In 1827 when
Kemble's acting company performed in Paris, Shakespeare (shunned as
the "aide-de-camp de Wellington" only five years previously) became a
favorite with the theater-going public and the mentor of painters
writers, and musicians. Then came the vogue for dandyism, horseracing
and English foods.[29] There were even quasi political extensions of the
coupling of Romanticism and Anglomania. Although the English were
notorious as cool and constrained, they were also known for their higher
degree of political liberty, which cast an indirect reflection of freedom
on things English. Just before the July Revolution when Charles X, who
had succeeded Louis XVIII in 1824, was trying to emulate the ab-
solutism of his ancestors, a French friend told Lady Morgan, "Everything English except their politics, is now, in Paris, popular, and is
deemed romantic; and we have romantic tailors, milliners, pastry-cooks,
and even doctors and apothecaries." [30]

With the overthrow of the Bourbons in 1830, painters used the thinly
veiled disguise of English history to attack them. Heine wrote of *Cromwell Contemplating the Remains of Charles I,* "Delaroche, by exhibiting
this picture, intended to call forth historical comparison . . . the paral-
lels between the errors and failings of the Stuarts and of the Bourbons,
and between the restorations in both countries. It is almost one and the
same story of rapid ruin." [31]

Painters also turned to a French national frame of reference in terms
of recent history. Many artists and revolutionaries hopefully recalled
the unrealized principle of 1789. The painting of an episode from the
days of the Gironde which Horace Vernet exhibited in the Salon of 1831
was a sort of substitute wish-fulfillment. It had a visual counterpart in

he appurtenances of real life. Heine observed that among its features
ere "those Terroristic waistcoats, with wide-spreading flaps, which
ave again become the fashion among Republican youths in Paris as
ilets à la Robespierre." [32]

As the regime of the Citizen King failed to fulfill expectations and,
n fact, engaged in repressive practices, French painters found it prac-
ically and psychologically difficult to treat contemporary themes other
han genre, portraits, and landscapes. After the 1820s, neither con-
emporary heroes nor protagonists seriously entered into fine art until
he advent of Courbet.

The political situation was not wholly responsible for the per-
istence of historical and allegorical themes, though in France, with the
ooperation of the art tradition, it prolonged their existence. Even in
England the old taste for allegory continued, often in timely contexts.
ames Ward's immense *Allegorical Painting of the Triumph of Water-
oo* was so involved that people could not understand it without the aid
f a lengthy descriptive pamphlet given away at the gallery where it
vas exhibited in 1821. There was also a public interested in properly
mpressive historical or Biblical pictures. Thus *Belshazzar's Feast* by
ohn Martin drew crowds so dense that it had to be railed off and the
xhibition extended for three additional weeks. But despite the penchant
f such painters as Martin, Turner, and Haydon for grandiose motifs,
English critics in the first two decades of the century deplored the general
aucity in English painting of subjects appropriate to High Art.[33]

The taste for a grandiose art, great in size as well as in subject, had
ever died out. Pictures tended to be heroic in size even though there
vas less architectural space than in the past to be filled—a traditional
mployment for art denied more often in England than in France. In
ne with persisting ideas of the grandeur of art and the cult of the
olossal which eighteenth-century theorists had made a quality of the
ublime, painters and public alike continued to desire large canvases.
These were felt to be as necessary for simple as for great or cosmic
ubjects. David Wilkie, Léon Cogniet, and Jean Gigoux gave large

dimensions to little anecdotes, making "machines" of the intimate. With his more profound themes, Blake was not satisfied with doing small engravings and watercolors; he also longed to execute decorative murals.[34] However, large canvases put a financial strain on artists. Constable's big landscapes, which were expensive to paint, did not sell well, and he admitted, "Painting those large pictures has much impoverished me [but I do not consider myself at work without I am before a six-foot canvas." [35]

The large physical size of paintings seemed to be related both to physical expansiveness intrinsic to human beings and to the loftiness of the sentiments they contained. Delacroix reflected with admiration of Gros's battle pieces and Géricault's *Medusa,* "The essential thing about these works is their reaching of the sublime, which comes in part from the size of the figures. The same pictures in small dimensions would, am sure, produce quite a different effect on me." [36]

The persistence of grandeur in art was not due merely to the idiosyncrasies of artists; it was in response to a living demand. In the 1830s and 1840s, while genre scenes remained popular, there was also a widespread desire for grand subjects as the numbers of middle class persons who aspired to an upper class style of life increased. The taste for grandeur did not, however, embrace the severe forms and didacticism of Davidian art. To persons in search of comfort rather than profound reforms, a solemn rendering of classical themes appeared distasteful or ridiculous. Even to painters, who wished a style that seemed more free or at least more relaxed, Davidian art seemed outdated. Thus when Gros tried to return to the sobriety of his master's style, many young artists mocked his *Humanity beseeching Europe in behalf of the Greeks* and *Hercules and Diomede,* exhibited a few months before his suicide in 1835. However, a more sensuous or vivacious rendering of themes from the ancient world through the Neoclassicism of Ingres or the Romanticism of Delacroix found many admirers.

At the same time, there was also a public for the grandeur of nonclassical—contemporary, historical, or allegorical—themes as well as styles. Thus English critics expressed enthusiasm for the "noble and elevated" art of the Frenchman Delacroix.[37] Even in his painting of *Liberty Leading the People,* exhibited in the Salon of 1831 along with more than forty other pictures dealing with the July Revolution, Delacroix gave meaning to actuality through allegory in the figure of Liberty

Lampooning the attempt at elevation in this second and last of Delacroix's paintings of a contemporary historical event, Heine wrote that the figure of Liberty reminded him "of those peripatetic female philosophers, those quickly-running couriers of love or quickly-loving ones, who swarm of evening on the Boulevards." [38] In this painting, the top-hatted young hero on the barricades (perhaps Delacroix, himself, in fantasy), clutching his musket among the dead and dying, casts his shadowed staring eyes for support, not to something tangible, but to an *idea* in the figure of Liberty which was soon to be betrayed. After the age of thirty-three, Delacroix devoted all his monumental works to historical, Biblical, mythological, or exotic themes, and in the 1840s and 1850s, even to classical subjects such as Marcus Aurelius and Heliodorus.

Often Delacroix tempered grandeur with more lyrical delights. As he wrote in his *Journal,* he concentrated on "those charming allegories of the Middle Ages and the Renaissance, those cities of God, those Elysian fields full of light, peopled with gracious figures, etc. . . . The soul rose ceaselessly above the trivialities and miseries of real life into imaginary dwellings which were embellished with everything that was lacking around you." [39] Feelings similar to Delacroix's may have nourished a popular taste for a mixture of costume romance and sentiment. It was as much in response to this taste as in reaction to a more profound dissatisfaction with himself that Wilkie in the 1830s preferred to paint medieval rather than contemporary episodes.[40]

Perhaps people in every type of society feel a sense of lack in some respect and need ideal or at least more exciting images to which they can appeal. Although the compensatory element in painting had also been present when art had stronger social ties, this aspect now began to usurp the field of interest. Disenchanted with some of its living reality, the public was attracted not only to realistic art dealing with its immediate, utilitarian world, but also to the historically remote and, as aristocrats and sophisticates of the middle class had been in the previous century, to the exotic. In the past also, artists had been interested in the strange and colorful designs and costumes of distant lands. Napoleon's commissions, however, focused painters' brushes on the glory of his North African campaigns rather than on the lives of the natives.

With the French penetration of North Africa in the duller, disillusioned 1830s, artists like Delacroix, Decamps, and Horace Vernet perceived and painted what they thought to be a simpler and more basic existence among primitive peoples—an idea present as early as Plato and reinvoked frequently throughout history. These painters did not actually settle in exotic lands, as Gauguin was to do among the Tahitians, nor derive inspiration from primitive or exotic art. For sensual stimulation or ideological compensation, they and the public would reinvoke exotic sights in their reveries. In the lives of remote peoples they could visualize an image of the idealized "natural" man.

Painters, as well as writers and musicians, also conveyed a sense of discontent and discomfiture with their immediate world in paintings of sea or desert—areas of alienation or escape but also of freedom and solitude, places in which to be lost or faced with boundlessness.[41] Small men are set in vast landscapes—safe and sound in the meadows of Constable, at peace in the leafy stillnesses of Corot and Rousseau and Huet, or dwarfed by the gigantic fanciful architecture of Martin, or swallowed up by the seas and storms of Turner. Two centuries distant from the sturdy merchant ships of the Dutch painters, men in small boats float on unstable waters, from the shipwrecked survivors of the *Medusa* to the frightened voyager through Hell on Dante's bark, to the legion of paintings of men in boats adrift which, far into the nineteenth century, covered the walls of exhibitions. As if in reference to the hazards surmounted by the great of Western history, Chenavard chose to depict in a boat his four heroes, Alexander, Caesar, Charlemagne, and Napoleon.

Though fascinating many artists and a considerable part of the public, precarious or exotic locales and remote heroes were not wholly satisfactory images in the life of the new society. As the ordinary man rose in social, economic, and political status, he looked for heroic figures who might be useful to him in his aspirations to a higher psychological status. Neither the commonplace William IV nor Louis Philippe would do; they seemed too much like the bourgeois himself, who wished to partake of the extraordinary.

Napoleon, however, served as a metaphor for greatness among all classes of people, including artists. In the Napoleonic vogue, which was at its zenith from 1827 to 1840, Delacroix saw one of the consequences of the democratic process. To him it seemed that "the ordinary man finds realized in Napoleon the ideal of the simple citizen who sees himself deserving to reach that high position where he can satisfy every kind of taste natural to a simple citizen. . . . He flatters himself with the thought that it is not impossible to attain all these pleasures, since one simple citizen did attain them." [42] Meissonier and many others painted the Napoleonic legend far into the century and, through prints, brought it into the humblest homes. While for many Napoleon became a symbol of the Revolution, more realistically he also served as a figure of authority and power. Thus Ure, whose book *Philosophy of Manufactures* appeared in 1836, praised Arkwright as a great man—"A man of Napoleon nerve and ambition, he knew how to impose the discipline of the factory upon an unruly mob." [43]

The transformation of the meaning of the hero who had traditionally stood for loftier ideals than those operative in daily life undermined his integrity and replaced him with a foot soldier in life's daily skirmishes. Meissonier's popular, precise delineations of episodes from Napoleon's campaigns are drained of the fire of the epic hero and animated by the image of men of restricted enterprise. At best, the new societies which, along with the ideal of individualism fostered a sense of loss of differentiation, were fallow ground for the old type of hero who had been defined in terms of distinctiveness from the mass.

By the time of Napoleon III in France and even earlier in England under the young Victoria, the hero, in painting as well as in literature, had been downgraded in social status or almost completely eclipsed.[44] In Daumier's painting *The Uprising,* there is an echo of the power of the strong-willed individual, but he is a common workman, arm raised and mouth opened to shout in the midst of a mob. Another kind of lower class protagonist emerged in the art and person of Courbet who, proclaiming that "to speak in a fashion different from all the world . . . is an aristocratic pose," proceeded to idealize himself as the realistic painter of peasants and workers.

Baudelaire mourned the passing of the heroic, even from landscape. He longed for "those great lakes, representing immobility in despair . . . immense mountains, staircases from our planet to the skies . . . castle keeps . . . crenellated abbeys, reflected in gloomy pools . . . gigantic bridges, towering Ninevite constructions, haunts of dizziness . . . everything, in short, which would have to be invented if it did not already exist." [45] When Thackeray wrote of English art in the 1840s, "The heroic has been deposed; and our painters are content to exercise their art on subjects far less exalted," [46] he was in fact explaining the emergence of a character that does not want to appear exceptional or unconventional, and that in Impressionist painting was to assume some of the most delightful of all images.

But the gradual democratization of the hero made possible the transference of qualities he had embodied to the artist himself and even to the ordinary man as carriers of truth, intensity, and the tragic character of the human condition—a process that in art later reached a climax in Expressionism. With their accession to the throne of the hero, they partook of his sufferings as well as his glory.

SEVEN

Love & Death

By intruding into the mind and emotions and by studying the body, the artist impinges on the territory of priest, psychotherapist, or physician. But rather than the counseling of love or prescribing against illness, his business and pleasure is the picturing of emotional and intellectual impacts and associations. More fundamentally, one of the pleasures of the painter is to exploit basic affects, to master primal drives and perhaps also to divest himself of aggression in the manipulation of his materials, through imagery and forms which his culture regards as art.

Some of the greatest artists have, in fact, asserted their love as well as hostility for humanity or the universe through violence of technique or theme. In Christian art they could blend the powers of love and death in the crucified Christ who died through love for mortals and triumphed over death in the Resurrection. As if in denial of the ultimate destination of death and the destruction of the body, the secular outlook and pagan themes of the Renaissance permitted an exposition of physical love as an affirmation of life. The passionate reformistic zeal of the Counter Reformation directed this sensualization into voluptuously painted martyrdoms of saints.

By the early eighteenth century, the artist who wished to portray glorious suffering or intense passionateness had almost no market. Under the new conditions of patronage which called for smaller and more intimate paintings, intensity or anguish seemed to have no place; they are, after all, uncomfortable to live with at home. Today, as well, the most sophisticated art lover might find even such a great but ghastly masterpiece as Grünewald's *Crucifixion* too painful to contemplate as he engages in small talk with friends or tries to enjoy a meal.

Nevertheless, pleasure-seeking French patrons in the early eighteenth century did not require joy in their art to be unadulterated. A taste for the touching, the sensitive, and the melancholic, which wafted through the intellectual and aristocratic classes, occasionally cast a shadow over the smiling face of Rococo art. But Watteau's painting and later the music of Mozart subordinated melancholy to a luminous enchantment. The sexually free aristocracy, taking passion lightheartedly, subsidized the art of delicate licentiousness painted by Boucher, whose boudoir pieces moved the late nineteenth-century writer Huysmans, apparently ignoring Chardin, to say that the Devil must have created the art of the eighteenth century as an insult to the Virgin Mary.

In Protestant England as well, there was a market among the Whig aristocracy, long after the brief fling of the Stuarts, for such paintings as the seduction scenes *Before* and *After,* patterned after French Rococo works, which the Duke of Montague commissioned from Hogarth. But artists usually depicted sexuality in an elliptical way in pictures destined for a clientele in whom the Puritan strain dominated. The triumphant female of the Rococo had an English counterpart in a type of picture in which the woman stands and the man sits, as if respectably to marry the poet and his muse.[1] But the tranquil and upright aspect of life that figures in this art, as well as in the genteel conversation piece, was not wholly representative of society in England which was known by foreign travelers as the "land of passion and catastrophe." [2] With its aristocratic Hell Fire clubs and its unruly and criminal street mobs, this society also called forth such cultural manifestations as the Riot Act, *The Beggar's Opera,* Jonathan Swift, and William Hogarth.

Hogarth's moralizing and didactic series of paintings of *A Harlot's Progress* and *A Rake's Progress* were an immediate success through engravings he resourcefully made of them in the 1730s for the purpose of making money. The first of a new class of pictures similar to popular plays combining morality and licentiousness which catered to all classes, they also exhibited the burgeoning social consciousness of the time. The first series seemed to reiterate Steele's earlier defense in *The Spectator* (1712) of prostitutes as victims of immorality in the large towns; the second satirized the middle class rake emulating the free sexual practices common among the Whig aristocracy. As Alexander Pope wrote in his *Moral Essays* the same year (1735) Hogarth's *Rake* appeared:

> *Whether the charmer sinner it or saint it,*
> *If folly grow romantic, I must paint it.*

Through the moral veil of punishment inflicted on the harlots and rakes, even the most virtuous lady or gentleman could enjoy vice and cruelty in art as much as could profligates in real life, especially in the greater privacy allowed by prints held in the hand over paintings hung on the wall.

Around the same time, salacious and satiric sentiments competed with a sentimentality that gushed forth in immensely popular novels like *Clarissa* in which Samuel Richardson preached and punished virtue.

With the revival of didactic academic painting in France, the wistful or playful eroticism, the light, flickering colors and movements, and the accent on youth of the Rococo were replaced by moral sobriety, a more somber coloration, and representation of the body as heavier, more mature. In 1750, only three years after Louis XV's minister of public works inaugurated an idealistic program for art, Rousseau attacked the mythological motifs in galleries and in public gardens as corruptive of public morals.[3] But as in England, morality was ambivalent. While Diderot praised "paintings inviting us to virtue," he wrote to Sophie Volland that passion and vice animate painting, poetry and music, and that virtue makes only cold pictures. One of his favorite painters, Greuze, seemed to incorporate both attitudes in his morally ambiguous subjects and figures—the falsely innocent child seductresses, the disobedient prodigal son and vengeful parental authority. In their exploitation of the feelings which amounted to self-deception about the nature of the feelings, these paintings give a foretaste of the sentimentality of some nineteenth-century art.

Rococo subjects, however, continued to be popular, and sometimes incorporated more serious along with sexually titillating intentions. The nobleman who commissioned Fragonard to paint *The Swing* in 1766 used a popular theme as a vehicle for anticlericalism. He directed the artist, who was bored with doing the sort of pictures the Academy wanted, to depict as a bishop the figure who sets the swing in motion, instigating the interplay of furling peek-a-boo skirt and libidinous glances.[4] What a contrast this picture makes with the domestically decorous portrayal of swinging in *Viscount Tyrconnel and His Family,* painted earlier in the century by Philippe Mercier who introduced French genre into England.[5]

By the 1770s, subjects concerned with the family, motherhood, childhood, and rustic life had become so popular in France that Fragonard joined Greuze in cultivating the new type of art. Even Boucher painted bourgeois interiors. The graver tone which the growing middle-class art public preferred—a taste which had infiltrated the aristocracy—was further promoted by a stepping-up of the official program when Louis XVI ascended the throne in 1774. The Comte d'Angiveller, who succeeded Marigny as commissioner of public works, eliminated "indecent and licentious little pictures" from the Salon.[6]

Boucher advised his young cousin and pupil David to work in the more serious vein if he wished to succeed. David gave a final blow to the Rococo with his desensualization of women in *The Oath of the Horatii,* in which he fully clothed their femininity and revealed their sorrow. In the context of a widespread reformistic mood in French society for many years before the Revolution, people hailed him as a "Messiah" and preferred him to contemporaries who also painted didactic ancient themes. His whole style, in form as well as content, seemed a more complete realization of that mood. In contrast with the physical and emotional relaxation in Rococo art, the labored composition and strained relationship between David's figures created a peculiar feeling of high tension, as if in resonance with the tenseness that accompanied the widely recognized social and personal dilemmas of the times.

With the open expression of violence in society during the Revolution and its subsequent disturbances, there mingled a stream of voluptuousness and of puritanism, often associated with revolutionaries as well as reformers. Replacing idyllic scenes of shepherds and shepherdesses, public festivals ennobled sensuality by incorporating it with ancient motifs and philosophical ideas. In one of these spectacles, Commissioners of the Senate drank water flowing from the breasts of a "Fountain of Regeneration." While festivals of the Revolution were lavish in their use of sensual symbols, streets were named Rue de la Temperance and Rue de la Frugalité in a secular spirit akin to that with which the English religious revolutionists of the seventeenth century had christened their children Praise God Barebone, Put-Thy-Trust-in-Christ, and Flee-Fornication Williams.[7] But even at the height of the Revolution, frivolous and sentimental tastes persisted: for instance, in novels called *Nouveau voyage sentimental* and *L'Amitié dangeureuse.*[8]

The passing of the exalted phase of the Revolution brought a relaxation in the moral atmosphere which, with its pretensions to virtue, often seemed more self-consciously licentious than in the Rococo period.

Thus during the Directory and the Consulat, Eliza and Lucien Bonaparte embarrassed their brother Napoleon, who insisted he was trying
to restore public decency, by posing clad only in flesh-colored tights for
some of the tableaux-vivants which represented Greeks and Romans as
living habitually in the fashion of classical sculpture.[9]

Constraints of the new morality persisted. David did not show the
rape in his painting of the *Sabine Women,* using instead the part of the
story which shows reconciliation between the warring parties as an
elliptical plea for forgiveness in post-Revolutionary France. In terms of
the old tradition, revived in the mid-eighteenth century, which had used
nudes as allegories of virtue, David's contemporary Prud'hon transformed still further the Rococo's carefree, witty love play into a dangerous game, fraught with sin and retribution in such pictures as *Innocence
Seduced by Love is Trapped by Pleasure, but she is followed by Repent-
ance who hides beneath the wing of the Seducer.*[10]

The stern mold of thought of the second half of the eighteenth
century, moralizing or sentimentalizing the erotic themes of art, cast
gloomy and often macabre shadows over the Rococo's revel with life
and ruffled the complacency of the conversation piece. The revival of
history painting reinvoked the image of death that had pervaded so much
seventeenth-century art.

Paintings of the deaths of Socrates and Seneca, absent from the
thematic repertoire for a century, began to appear frequently in France
around 1750. Diderot admired a melodramatic picture of 1761 as a
"composition filled with terror," in which Diomede "casts a terrifying,
haughty, ferocious glance on a pile of corpses; the slaughter continues
around him, the blood gushing out and staining the waters of the
Xanthu." [11]

While the spectacle of death in some of the death scenes is a sort of
sensual analog, historical characters are often sanctified as secular martyrs
whose sufferings are not only the sign but also the condition of greatness.
Self-sacrificing ancient heroes had already been idolized under Louis XV.
Between 1775 and 1785, there was a considerable increase in the number

of paintings that depicted great men, generally Biblical or Greek or Roman, at the moment of their death.[12] By the early 1780s, artists were also painting the death scenes of medieval or Renaissance personages, such as Ménageot's painting of Leonardo da Vinci on his deathbed. Contemporary heroes and celebrities were also honored. Vien did an *Apotheosis of Winckelmann;* David painted the murdered patriots Le Pelletier-Saint Fargeau and Marat and the child martyr Viala in quiet beatification, as if on sacrificial altars, and, in accord with classical tragedies of the stage, not showing the acts that had caused their deaths.

Painters did not remove all the suffering from common experience by embodying it in idealized settings. In England, where the tragic tradition was not as firmly established in painting, the transition from ritual to reality came about considerably earlier. With the change in status and locale of the hero that set in with the *Death of Wolfe,* recently dead or contemporaneous heroes were deified by death or pain. The patron of *Watson and the Shark* (which was to serve Géricault as a model for his *Medusa* forty years later) ordered Copley to paint him at the moment of agony: by suffering magnificently, he assumed the attributes of traditional classical heroes.

Placing the hero in extreme situations and qualifying his grandeur were, in fact, compatible with classical theory. A favorite topic of argument in artistic circles in the mid-eighteenth century was the question whether, in the famous Hellenistic statue, Laocoön cries out or merely groans in his anguished struggle against the fatal serpents. (Winckelmann said the figure showed admirable Greek restraint because he groans.)

Whether the observer was, in fantasy or unconsciously, inflicting or suffering pain, in accord with the ancient cathartic function of tragedy, cannot be ascertained. But the "seeksorrow," ancestor of the modern "masochist," was well-known to the people of the time; and the existence of the sadist was scandalously revealed by the Divine Marquis.

Beginning in the mid-eighteenth century, shadowy pleasures were exploited on a wider scale in painting through almost all areas of subject matter, including ruins, shipwrecks, storms, and battles. Somewhat earlier prints had catered to a general interest in shipwreck scenes[13] which may have been stimulated by the increase in sea travel, still so

Courtesy of the Detroit Institute of Arts

Fuseli, *The Nightmare*, 1781-82

hazardous in those days. Burke's contention that "the great ought to be dark and gloomy," consonant with classical tenets, helped spread the taste to more elevated artistic and social spheres. Idealized morbidity was enshrined in the gardens of the wealthy. One of the finest late eighteenth-century gardens, at Mr. Tyers' house at Denbies, had a Valley of the Shadow of Death with skulls scattered picturesquely about and coffins instead of columns.[14] Seeking a "Gothic" painter to execute a gruesome and uncanny "Gothic" picture for him, Horace Walpole's nephew Lord Orford chose Fuseli, whom a poet eulogized as "the genius of horror and romantic awe." [15]

As in so many other areas of subject matter and technique, the English—in whom continentals professed to find a heavy melancholia so characteristic that they called it *le mal anglais*—had a priority on themes of horror and violence in painting as well as in the Gothic tale and graveyard poetry. *Death on the Pale Horse,* which Benjamin West painted in 1817, in its violence seems a preview of Delacroix. In James Ward's *The Serpent of Ceylon,* which showed a boa constrictor winding himself around a Negro on a horse, there was a studied cruelty matching and perhaps surpassing that in any contemporary French painting, some thirty years before Delacroix's animal combats. The interest of some artists in necrophilic and sadistic themes considerably antedated their appearance in finished paintings, which awaited the public's toleration of such subjects as material for High Art. Thus West had made a sketch for *Death on the Pale Horse* twenty years before he executed the picture.[16]

The long period of foreign wars, uneasy intermittent periods of peace, and internal civil disturbances, real and feared, provided a general atmosphere and concrete occasions for the proliferation of such art. In alleged and real atrocities of the opening years of the nineteenth century, cruel and monstrous imagery—which had existed in popular prints, especially in England, and surpassed in extravagance nearly everything produced in High Art[17]—found a fresh field for exploitation. Unlike the pain inflicted by the tumults of nature, this imagery reproduced suffering avoidable in that it derived from a "human nature" dehumanized by the sleep of reason that unleashes the monsters of war, more fiendish than the demons in Fuseli's erotic *Nightmare.*

After David's quietly dignified martyrs, there arrived in the large canvases of the Empire images which seem to shriek with the infliction and endurance of pain in spectacles of men and horses rushing over body-strewn battle fields. While artists painted the Emperor dominating the scene (and himself?) as he wished, calm on a fiery white horse, they also dwelt in gruesome detail on wounded soldiers who did not bear their trials so stoically but writhed and grimaced in torment in the panoramic display of glory and gore.

Upon Napoleon's deposition, a new specter of death appeared in art, stripped of the trimmings of military glory or the old type of glorification through idealization. In the new imagery, struggle, suffering, and death seem to be enjoyed for themselves alone.

For Frenchmen under the Empire, there still seemed to be something worth dying for. "Death herself was beautiful then," wrote Musset in his *Confession d'un enfant du siècle*, "so great, so magnificent . . . there were only cadavers or demigods." Then, with the gods dethroned and under conditions of frustration, aggression against others frequently became aggression against the self, and thus symbolically against others. One could at least execute the grand gesture of suicide. Histories do not mention suicide epidemics in France during the Revolution and the Empire when opportunities for overt action were plentiful. They cluster from 1798 to 1804 under the Directory and the Consulate, and after 1815 and 1830.[18] History records numerous suicides among artists, evoked perhaps by the sufferings of *Werther*. While the rate of suicide and insanity, among artists and nonartists, may or may not have increased during the period, as Dr. Georget said (and we can never know), the belief of many contemporaries that this was so does reflect a widespread concern with the disastrous consequences of situations in which aspirations may be aroused on a grand scale only to be thwarted. And surely the "armed peace" [19] that pervaded the pre-Empire years, the Restoration, and the July monarchy did not funnel organic tendencies toward action, but encouraged other kinds of aggression or dwelling on disaster and death.

After the Empire, a taste for the morbid in painting often appeared in the form of melancholy, which already had entered literature in Chateaubriand. Melancholy now became intensified into depression or despair. "Napoleon dead, divine and human authorities were indeed reestablished, but belief in them no longer existed," reminisced Musset. "At the same time that outer life was so pallid and shabby, the inner life of society took on a somber and silent aspect." Delacroix expressed a similar sense of desolation in the pathetic frightened girls in cemeteries he painted in 1823—a new variation on eighteenth-century elegiac poetry of the graveyard and the idyllic paintings of Hubert Robert, who showed contemporary peasants among classical ruins. Preoccupied with the tragic man who suffers from the conflict between his aspirations and inner or outer limitations, Delacroix and other artists painted and drew such melancholic and rebellious figures as Hamlet, Werther, Faust and Don Quixote, sometimes with their own visages.

Often the taste for morbidity was still more extreme. In the first monumental Romantic painting in France, necrophily was as much the attraction as disaster was the subject. Géricault was so concerned with the faithful rendering of dead and decaying flesh of the people in *The Raft of the Medusa,* that he made many painstaking preliminary studies of the limbs of corpses he acquired from the medical school. Response was mixed to the finished painting. Ingres expressed revulsion for the *Medusa* and "those other paintings of the amphitheater which only show us man as a cadaver, which only reproduce the ugly, the hideous; no, I'll have none of them!" [20] Although other Frenchmen regarded it so highly that it was purchased by the state, the picture was not hung because of its political implications, so that the disgusted artist retrieved it and exhibited it in England where its propaganda went unnoticed.[21] A British critic, no doubt imbued with a taste for "Gothic" horror, admired its "charmed Melancholy." [22] Years later Ruskin passed moral judgment on the *Medusa:* "I think it is the strangest curse and corruption which attends humanity, but it is a quite inevitable one, that wherever there is a ruthless pursuit of sensational pleasure, it always ends in an insane and wolf-like gloating over the garbage of death." Apparently this defender of sublime art could not tolerate sublime horror, not even for long in the *Slave Ship* (1840) by his idol Turner, which became so painful to live with that he sold this paternal gift a few years after his father's death.[23]

Although the *Medusa* was the fruition of a long European tradition and inaugurated a new form of its expression, some of the most advanced paintings of the period, in conception and technique, were completely uncolored in subject and pigment with the tones of death and decay. The same year that Géricault exhibited the *Medusa,* Constable painted *The White Horse,* "one of my happiest efforts on a large scale, being a placid representation of a serene gray summer morning." Constable tried to evade the terrible and the openly sensual, blending the two as a single object of condemnation. However tame they may seem in comparison with the paintings of his successors, David's *Bonaparte Crossing the Alps, Mars and Venus,* and the *Death of Marat* repelled Constable when he saw them in London in 1834. "They are indeed loathsome," he said. "David seems to have formed his mind from three sources, the scaffold, the hospital, and a brothel." [24] Probably Constable would have been even more shocked if he had seen the fully developed type, drenched in passion without compassion, in *The Death of Sardanapalus* which Delacroix based on Byron's poem, displaying the nude harem being slain on the doomed potentate's bier.

While attraction to themes of torment or self-torment was not universal among Romantic painters, many felt drawn to an art imagery of strongly aggressive sensations, in which they or the spectator were immediately or intimately involved. In order to experience for himself the fury of the elements which he painted in *Steamer in a Snowstorm* and as if to assert man's victory over nature, Turner had himself lashed to the mast, as Joseph Vernet had done in the previous century. The turbulent atmospheric effects and deluges painted by Girodet, Joshua Shaw, and other early nineteenth-century artists were perhaps most highly dramatized in John Martin's cascading waters and lightning flashing on jagged mountain peaks, which earned him praise and the sobriquet, "Mad Martin."

In their figure pieces, the young French Romantics also believed that strife and pain with which the spectator could identify himself were necessary for the animation of the images of art. The ancients might still be frames of reference, not in their late eighteenth-century stoic forms but, according to *Le Globe* in 1825, when they were shown as "men like ourselves who feel all the affections of humanity. . . . Hercules, Philoctetus, Prometheus suffer and wail freely and they are not for that reason any the less heroes and gods." [25] Intensifying and extending pre-Revolutionary trends, the Romantics depicted heroism in terms of the infliction of pain in their medieval and Renaissance assassination themes, through the endurance of pain, as in the *Medusa,* or through a combination of the two, as in *The Death of Sardanapalus.*

The imagery of aggression was sometimes coupled with themes of the violation of the flesh. Delacroix told himself, "Remember eternally certain passages from Byron to inflame your imagination for all time. They suit me well. The end of *The Bride of Abydos, The Death of*

Selim, his body tossed by the waves . . . *The Death of Hassan* in *The Giaour.* The Giaour contemplating his victim and the curses of the Mussulman on the murderer of Hassan. The description of Hassan's deserted place. The vultures whet their beaks before the conflict. The grapplings of the warriors who seize each other. In doing which one dies, biting the arm of his enemy." [26]

Animal imagery often served as a vehicle of concealment for human aggression and sensuality. The Romantics used animals both to disguise and to heighten emotionality by referring, as writers had done at least since the seventeenth century, to uncontrollable impulses in human beings in terms of their resemblances to animal anarchy. The Neoclassicists, stressing the ordering power of reason as supreme in man, had seldom used animals in their paintings. When David placed an unbridled horse—a symbol of passion, and unleashed!—in *The Rape of the Sabine Women,* he was mocked. David's pupils, however, had occasion to give a prominent role to animals in their military canvases. In the next generation, Delacroix wrote with relish of Gros's *Battle of Aboukir,* "He knows how to paint the sweat which inundates the croups of his horses in the midst of battle, and almost the flaming breath which comes from their nostrils." [27]

Géricault extricated the dashing forms of horses from a military milieu, employing the action and passion they represented in other contexts. Delacroix's white horse thrashing in a storm seems a symbol of terror. This theme had been anticipated in 1770 by the English specialist in animal anatomy, George Stubbs, in his *White Horse Frightened by a Lion,* a scene he was said to have witnessed in Morocco, where Delacroix also was to observe many exciting episodes.

Delacroix, in particular, excelled in intertwining human and animal forms and qualities in his combats between animals and between animals and men. In works reminiscent of the grisly *Milo of Cortona* carved by Puget some one hundred fifty years earlier, Delacroix depicted a tiger sinking teeth or claws into the neck of a man or the breast of a woman. It is as though he were reaffirming an ancient belief that beasts, like savages, are more "natural" and hence man's superior. By the identification of man and beast, as with the high valuation he placed on fantasy, he seemed to assert a more modern view by locating the excellence of man in many traits which had often been regarded as abnormalities.[28] Indeed, the

Romantics developed a modern gallery of bestiaries which served as metaphors in life as well as in art. Keats liked to use the terms "proud steed," "lion," "eagle," "tiger," "dove."

As animal metaphor and imagery often served as symbol or disguise, so also an attraction to cruelty might be concealed by a bland façade. So widespread was a taste for the contemplation of suffering and pain that even in the popular sentimental pictures it was sometimes the framework of communication. In a piece like Wilkie's *The Cut Finger,* everyone could enjoy a mild sort of suffering without being overly pained. Or one could weep—for tears were not banned for men until the second half of the century—at such paintings as Wilkie's *A Sick Lady Visited by Her Physician.* Through the conversion of suffering into sentimentality, one could enjoy the sight and the sensation without the risk of moral condemnation attached to the sensual themes with which it was often blended.

Fascination with pain and death was not restricted to artists. Although people did not live—in spite of the wars and sporadic outbreaks of typhoid—on such intimate terms with death as in the centuries when the Plague had carried off large proportions of the population, they continued to ceremonialize and enshrine it. In the cities of the dead of the new urban societies, the cemeteries which mushroomed in the 1830s, persons of the middle class could enjoy the same kind of tomb formerly inhabited by the great. Imagery of death and the macabre abounded also among the festive occasions of the living. At one of the costume balls of the 1830s, the stairway of the house was decorated with weeping willows, and a servant in red livery ushered guests into a somber room called the Salon of Melancholy where hung paintings of a Nightmare, an Expedition of Vampires, and the Massacre of Chios. Among the guests were *le Bel Obscur, le Mélancholique,* and *le Terrible* of whom it was said, "Nobody paints better than he the decomposition of cadavers and the phenomena of putrefaction." [29] Appropriately, Thomas de Quincey wrote a humorous essay on *Murder Considered as one of the Fine Arts.*

Whether in jest or in serious art, imagery of death, terror, and suffering prevailed as open and even sanctioned cruelty in life was more curtailed. Primarily, the inhibition affected the conscience as changes in the social structure made for the wider dissemination of humanitarian and other values of the Enlightenment. Savage as the laws and practices of those times seem against the more subtle cruelties of our day— practices Géricault recorded in his studies of public executions and the heads of guillotined and hanged men—there was a progressive softening of the penal code, and in England a growth of philanthropy, from the formation of an Association for Improving the Situation of Infant Chimney-Sweepers in 1803 to a great increase in charities in the 1830s.

As the new ideas and prohibitions affected all classes, even people of high and middle class society continued to be attracted to the lower sentiments associated with the lower classes, as they had also in Hogarth's day. In addition, they feared their social inferiors as incompatible with excellence and subversive of order, like Tobias Smollett's Squire Bramble who declared in his novelistic travels of 1770, "The mob is a monster I never could abide, either in its head, tail, midriff, or members; I detest the whole of it, as a mass of ignorance, presumption, malice, and brutality." Despite its social and intellectual refinements and the decline of such entertainments as bull-baiting and cockfighting in the 1820s and 1830s, the Swell Mob continued to enjoy excursions to public executions, which were not abolished in England until 1868.[30] Nevertheless, a sense of guilt, reinforced by the newly pervasive moral condemnation of overt cruelty, may actually have increased its attractiveness in the more removed sphere of art. The priority of an imagery of cruelty and terror in English painting may also be connected with the earlier formation of a social structure that accommodated and disseminated the new appeals to conscience as well as the new morality in general.

Thus animals continued to play a more prominently substitutive role in English painting, as they had also in those eighteenth-century pictures in which animals served as moral allegories (as in Hogarth's *Four Stages of Cruelty*), or pictures in which playfulness was manifested in sporting scenes rather than in love play. Particularly in the works of Landseer, they were humanized as bearers of a philosophic, sentimental, or moral message. Landseer's dogs were English nineteenth-century allegorical figures, evading the sensual female allegories which had long prevailed in France. The female nude was so standard in French art that Granet joked, thinking perhaps of his old friend Ingres who excelled in the genre, about a project he had in 1840 for painting, not a nude as was the fashionable practice of the day, but a well-covered monk, with only head and finger tips showing.[31]

No English artist before William Etty, a contemporary of Ingres, specialized in painting the female nude. When nudes occurred in English art, their sensuality was disguised in the context of "great" or "moral" subject matter, or in the frigidity of the plaster cast *à l'antique*. A more acceptable type of admiration for women was to be found in Lawrence's languishing ladies and Opie's timid blushing girls and his popular *Lovesick Maid*—women who must be protected or manipulated by men, but who must be shielded from the open expression of carnality.

An almost frantic reverence for women was shown in England at the same time that the evils of sex were branded by religious Perfectionism.[32] Protectiveness extended to their images as well as their persons: there were strong objections when James Ward's *The Serpent of Ceylon* was hung between two portraits of ladies.[33] People realized that the English religious heritage aggravated sensual taboos. Thus Crabb Robinson, one of Blake's admirers, wrote from Germany in 1804, "To express what we should call Puritanism in language, and excess of delicacy in matters of physical love, the word Engländerei has been coined." [34]

Etty felt obliged to defend his works, inspired by Raphael, from indignant attacks, such as that of a critic rejecting his *Youth on the Prow and Pleasure at the Helm* as "another indulgence of what we once hoped a classical, but which we are now convinced is a lascivious mind . . . no decent family can hang such sights against their walls. The naked female may, in the severity of the antique, be modest, but it is not so in the attitudes of Mr. Etty." [35] The painter insisted that his work was supremely moral and that, for instance, the underlying idea of his *Sirens,* exhibited the same year Victoria became queen, was " 'The Wages of Sin is Death.' People may think me lascivious, but I have never painted with a lascivious motive." He justified his art in terms of chasteness of principle: "Finding God's most glorious work to be Woman, that all human beauty had been concentrated in her, I resolved to dedicate myself to painting—not the Draper's or Milliner's work,—but God's most glorious work, more finely than had ever been done." [36]

Lack of sexual frankness was not restricted to England. And of course, sexual attitudes and practices have never been completely free but are subject to taboos which, in some form or other, in all cultures, have been deemed necessary for the preservation and conduct of personal and social life. In the early nineteenth century, social changes directed certain aspects of the Judaeo-Christian heritage into more constrictive channels in Catholic as well as Protestant countries. Thus Sainte-Beuve in *Volupté* speculated on his own conflicts in adolescence during the Restoration, "Such excessive bashfulness resembles a sickness: this superstitious sense of shame makes things seem reprehensible." However, sensuality in the French art tradition was a bulwark against its suffocation in painting by the newly pervasive morality which in the past had been more or less restricted to the middle class. In continuation of a process visible in the early eighteenth century, morals as well as other aspects of life became bourgeois among more sectors of society, approximating the already existing English situation. By the 1830s the open practice of adultery, which had allowed sexual freedom to women as well as to men in high (as in low) society, was no longer countenanced.

The new moral relationship between the sexes created a disturbance in the social image of the woman that was strongly accented by double reactions of respect and hostility. A social separation between men and women, entirely foreign to the eighteenth-century salon, was noticed by the French painter Mme. Vigée-Lebrun when she returned to Paris from exile after the Revolution. At an important party she found, reminiscent of English custom, the innovation of men gathering on one side of the room and women on the other, "like hostile forces, you would have said . . . Not a man came over to our side excepting the master of the house." [37]

The same dominant groups that effected a social separation between the sexes, presumably to protect women, proceeded to subordinate them in the interests of the new economic and political system. The Civil Code contained elaborate precautions to buttress paternal authority in the family, which was one of the few remaining secure social institutions in France. Answering to ideals of duty, virtue, and property rights, it disavowed, in the name of liberty, the greater freedom of relationships between men and women under the old regime. The new orientation was formulated by Bonald, who believed "the public authority should be,

like domestic authority . . . one, masculine, proprietary, perpetual, because, without unity, without masculinity, without property, there is no
real independence." [38]

Under the bourgeois July monarchy, Madame Ancelot complained
that the club had been substituted for the salon.[39] As if to symbolize the
new stress on masculine authority as opposed to feminine, fashion made a
sharper differentiation between the sexes than in the eighteenth century,
instituting the black frock coat as a masculine uniform in contrast with
the greater freedom permitted women in costume which was denied them
in life.

From the internal war against basic desires, an ambiguous composite
ideal emerged in the light of expectations that women should be Ma-
donnalike and alluring pagan goddesses, fragile sylphs and dangerous
temptresses like Medea and the Furies. Modernizing, with a vengeance,
the medieval battle between love and chastity in the *Roman de la Rose,*
the new code made women seem creatures to be both cherished and
destroyed. Young men would address their "pure" beloved with the same
invocations that had been used for the Madonna. At the same time, love
seemed a crime in which both parties must be punished. Not only was
love a painful sentiment; pain was a condition of its fulfillment, as exposed to extremes by the Marquis de Sade. Transforming eighteenth-
century sentimental tears into dreadful passionateness, a French girl
wrote to her lover in 1839, "With you suffering itself is a voluptuous
pleasure," almost as an echo of Saint-Beuve's words to George Sand,
"Love means tears; if you weep, you love."

By the 1830s, in elaboration of the aerial appearance so fashionable
under the Directory, women were supposed to look fragile and languishing, and to avoid lively movements which might make them appear guilty
of spontaneous gaiety. *La Mode* observed, "At the present time, all our
days resemble English or American Sundays. A woman would cause a
scandal if, at a ball, she did not walk like a boneless ghost." If a woman
wished to have the highly esteemed *air poitrinaire*—it was considered
"common" to have rosy cheeks or a healthy appearance—she could coax
it by eating lemons by the dozen, drinking vinegar, painting the face
green, and using belladonna or atropine; she could acquire deep brooding
shadows under the eyes by reading all night even if she had little interest in books. But her pallor must be ardent and impassioned, a trans-
parency for the storms that raged within.

Following and coexisting with the dependent creature who was an object of worship and sadism, was the vogue for the independent and aggressive woman, the "lioness" à la George Sand, the enigmatic and dangerous woman. The deep, fixed glance, vaporous air, humid eyes and disordered hair were not only signs of passion and inspiration; they were the hallmarks of the "disturbing woman," the "fatal and damned creature" who was at once charming and dangerous. A young painter wrote to his beloved in 1835 in terms that might describe Delacroix's *Medea* preparing to murder her children, which was exhibited at the Salon three years later, "On your deathly pale skin the light plays in violet and greenish reflections. Your teeth gleam like those of a young tigress, and your eyes have a strange brightness, a brightness which terrifies me. Only an angel or a devil can have such glances." [40]

In painting there were reflections of the ambiguous social image of the woman—far more ambiguous even than in Greuze's time. By the early nineteenth century, the gay, triumphant feminine world in Rococo art was shattered, or at least heavily veiled, or subject to penalties for the man. Two apparently different kinds of woman appeared in art after her desensualization in the *Horatii:* the innocent, submissive type and the sensual, dangerous type. The woman as menace was celebrated, for instance, in the figure of Medea, cloaked in the Neoclassical forms of Cherubini's opera or in the more tempestuous ones of Delacroix's and Turner's canvases. Even in the 1750s and 1760s, English and French artists had painted the sorceress, though as Carle Van Loo pictured her, not in a paroxysm of rage but at a "sublime" moment, just as he also showed Apollo and Laocoön dominating their passions, in order to reveal "a great and tranquil soul." When Turner's painting of Medea was exhibited at the Royal Academy in 1831, "raving in the midst of her bedevilments and incantations," many considered it quite "mad." [41]

But generally the woman was subdued, naturally or forcibly, in the forms and themes of late eighteenth- and early nineteenth-century painting, whatever the specific style. Delacroix used the theme of violation of the flesh not only in his animal combats, but also in a violence against women which amounted to delight in the spectacle of their anguish in such paintings as *The Death of Sardanapalus* and *The Abduction of Rebecca.* The sentiment was present already in the young painter who wrote ecstatically of his *Massacre of Chios,* "O smile of the dying! The look of the mother's eyes! Embraces of despair, precious domain of painting!" [42] In England, Haydon also delighted at the sight of the agonized woman. He was pleased to find as a model for the expression of the mother in his *Solomon* a woman who had just seen her son dashed to pieces by a horse: "Nothing could exceed her dreadful suffering." [43]

Subjugation of the woman also took place in the rendition of bodily forms. Ingres' women are placid. They humbly supplicate men, as Thetis does Jupiter in the famous painting, or they lie or stand in docile postures, not invitingly as in the Renaissance or coquettishly as in the Rococo. Immobilized women were not a Neoclassical monopoly. Something of the same torpor can be seen in many of the female figures painted by Romantics and artists close to them. Delacroix's harem women, as well as the nudes of Ingres, represent an odalisque type whose languorous passivity, seductive yet aloof, is remote from the actively enticing, happy mistresses of the Rococo. They appear not just passive in an alluring sense but, as in the works of Chassériau and later of the Pre-Raphaelites, actually immobilized by the discrepancy between their bodies and their indifferent heads which seem too weak to will to move the heavy limbs. When they move, they are sometimes frantic, or they become fragile phantoms as in the canvases of Corot's dematerialized style, reminiscent of the sylphs in Lamartine's poems. In the works of Etty and Chassériau, there is a disquieting incongruity between the voluptuous bodies and poses and the melancholic or virtuous heads.

Standards of beauty were also varied and ambiguous. There was no consensus of opinion as to what constituted feminine beauty, even within the same generation of artists who belonged to the same "school." Neither Balzac nor Hugo found Delacroix's women attractive. Hugo thought Delacroix had never painted a beautiful woman with the exception of one in *The Apparition of the Angels* in the Church of Saint-Paul and the female torso in *The Massacre of Chios.* "He has expression," the writer said, "but he does not have the ideal. The *Women of Algiers,* for example, that oriental glitter of light and color, are of the type of exquisite ugliness that belongs to the feminine creations of Delacroix." [44]

The Metropolitan Museum of Art, New York. Wolfe Fund, 1903

Delacroix, *The Abduction of Rebecca*, 1846

But in the art of Girodet and other painters working in the early years of the century, a more extreme deformation of the nude had occurred, sometimes with fantastic proportions, but svelte in general aspect. As continued into the 1860s in the art of Ingres, the elegant nude became a new *beau idéal,* blending sensuality and tranquillity. Just as there was a strong attraction to a coloration which, Ingres claimed, "leaves the

Ingres, *The Turkish Bath*, 1859

The Louvre, Paris. Archives photographiques

spirit calm,"[45] so also was there a receptivity for the simpler forms he patterned after the generally less turbulent art of Raphael which, however, were exciting in their sinuous outlines.

The attachment to Ingres' style as a source of calm and spirituality, as well as sensual excitement, hints at the ambivalent nature of the taste for his art. It was in accord with what Tocqueville called "that discreet, well-regulated sensualism, which prevails today." [46] Indeed, the art public of the 1840s and 1850s admired, along with Ingres' nudes, the saturnalia paintings which, like the masked balls, were socially approved channels for the forbidden. Even the tightly packed gathering of female nudes in *The Turkish Bath* which Ingres painted in his eighties, in which poses range from the seductive to the homosexual, was received with plaudits by a public and critics whose counterparts in England had been scandalized by Etty's "debasing sensuality."[47]

In these paintings, as in the works and words of Etty, in the disguised voluptuousness of keepsake pictures, and later in the anti-sin paintings of the Pre-Raphaelites, there is illustration for Blake's contention in his long poem *Vala* that the worship of chastity, which he regarded as sex repressed, amounts to the worship of sex itself.

> *And Urizen laid the first Stone, & all his myriads*
> *Builded a temple in the image of the human heart.*
> *And in the inner part of the Temple, wondrous workmanship,*
> *They form'd the Secret place, reversing all the order of delight,*
> *That whosoever enter'd into the temple might not behold*
> *The hidden wonders, allegoric of the Generations*
> *Of secret lust, when hid in chambers dark the nightly Harlot*
> *Plays in Disguise whisper'd hymn & mumbling prayer. . . .*

In the trappings of stories from the scriptures, violently sensual themes were well received in English painting, though often more elliptically than in France. What a contrast John Martin's portrayal in his *Fall of Nineveh* of the death of Sardanapalus and his concubines makes with the same theme which Delacroix painted a year earlier! While in Martin's picture the victims are discreetly draped, tiny figures, engulfed by landscape and architecture, their great nude bodies flood Delacroix's canvas. The Sardanapalus of the French painter reclines impassively as if a Moloch presiding at a sacrificial rite. Martin's potentate stands as if animated by high purpose. According to the exhibition catalog of 1828, he "cannot yield himself to the mock of the triumphant rebels; he cannot abandon his beloved women to their embraces; he goes with them to voluntary death rather than drag on a life of degradation."[48] So standard did such themes become as exhibition pieces that even the gentle Corot, in the hope of obtaining official recognition, sub-mitted a *Burning of Sodom* to the Salon in 1843.

The most sensational mid-century works referring to sensual in-dulgence were eclectic in style, such as *Young Venetian after an Orgy* and *Romans in the Decadence of the Empire* which, though probably in-spired by Bulwer's popular novel *The Last Days of Pompeii,* Couture painted, with ironic appropriateness, shortly before the inauguration of the Second Empire. To us, these orgiastic paintings look as ridiculous in their extravagances as many a canvas of the magnificent nude Prometheus being dashed on a rock by cataclysmic waves. For, as Dela-croix said, "The terrible in the arts is a natural gift like that of grace. The artist who is not born to express that sensation and who wants to attempt it is even more ridiculous than the one who attempts lightness despite a lack of it in his nature. . . . The terrible is like the sublime; it is not to be abused." [49]

Perhaps like the writers who frequently used such words as "orgy" and "adultery," the public of the "golden mean" also felt nostalgic for certain freedoms of the Rococo world which they did not permit them-selves to retain in life as heirs of the old aristocracy. Of course, the freer habits of earlier days persisted among individuals of all classes in both France and England. Victoria herself was not as puritanical as many of her contemporaries: for instance, she was not shocked by but openly admired and wished to purchase one of Mulready's nude studies in 1853 which the directors of the art school of the Royal Academy had been warned against letting her see. [50]

Indeed, aggressively sensual themes reached new heights of popularity in painting as the middle class became established in its new position of moral as well as political authority. Thus sensual and sadomasochistic pictures were imagery of the middle class as well as of artists who were antagonistic to many middle class values. Indeed, Etty's principal clients were merchants. He became the first English painter to specialize in the female nude, as the free-living-and-loving habits of the fashionable circles of the Regency waned with the ascendancy of that combination of vigor and constraint which came to be known as Victorianism. For while many Englishmen verbally castigated themselves for being a prudish nation, they shunned workaday taboos in their fantasy or their art. Thus, at the Victorian era's zenith, Redgrave in his *Century of*

Painters (1866) praised Fuseli, forty-one years after his death, as an artist who "always carries us away into a poetic region of his own—a region apart from the everyday world in which we live. . . . It is at least a dream-land in which we awaken to sublime thoughts and curious pleasures. . . ."

A veiling of impulses denied socially acceptable outlets, the popular renditions of sensuality and violence in both England and France did not spring from the free emotionality of the individual, according to the Romantic ideal. They were preludes to the slickly contrived, pseudo chaste, photographically explicit nudes which became so fashionable in the works of Bouguereau and other eclectic and academic artists in the second half of the century.

And so the weakening of intensity did not occur only in Delacroix's art as he grew older, nor in Romanticism. In fact, Delacroix, perhaps because he possessed the "natural gift," was able to sustain Romanticism in painting longer than its other early adepts in France who fell away in the 1830s. Although in the confluence of the new ideas about art and artists, painters theoretically were free to change the stringencies of the old tradition which had begun to collapse in the previous century, they were rarely able to function, because of outer and inner circumstances, in accord with their original high expectations.

When favorable atmospheric conditions failed to materialize, men with global ideals who had adopted painting as a vocation drifted away from Romanticism in France, and from painting itself in the more inhospitable clime of England, where the earlier maturity of Romantic art was followed by its untimely death. But in France, the stronger traditional supports for painting sustained the further development of the new artistic ideas and practices into the successive styles of modern art which, despite their relatively autonomous status, are inseparably a part of modern life.

EIGHT

Conclusion

With a shift to isolated institutions and private buyers as its mainstay, modern art is not, as often lamented, divorced from the social order. It is wedded for better and worse to the same world that nurtures constant change and inconstancy of taste and attachment.

An essential part of that world, for the painter, is the sphere of art. For no matter how original an artist may be, the nature of contemporary art circumscribes the further development of his inventiveness and the dissemination of his style. Even in the more remote past when it had some special purpose as a medium of magic or as a means of recording and teaching religion or history, art had other aspects as well, which were not brought into the center of interest until a later date. For instance, the delightful little figures that scamper in the foliate borders of medieval manuscripts dealing with sacred texts were confined to the borders. Chardin painted his tranquil canvases while the Rococo style of art and life was still in vogue; since he was over fifty at the time, he could not have been influenced by the mid-eighteenth century revival of classicism which promoted a different type of art; but he did not have followers. The spotting of color that characterizes Impressionism was already present, not only in Constable and Delacroix, but almost two hundred years earlier in Velásquez, who used it, however, only in a marginal way, subsidiary to what were believed to be more important aspects of art at that time.

Marginal elements within art do not finally become dominant and coalesce into a style by pure chance or by an ineluctable immanent process. It was not absolutely necessary that those particular styles should have been formed: the complexity of the Western art tradition afforded many alternatives for selection. Since changes occurred even in naturalistic or realistic art long after "realism" had been mastered, it is clear that they were not due to genetic tendencies toward representational accuracy. Because of the greater freedom of selection for artists and viewers as art became more separated from other social institutions, and because of the formation of various publics within the whole population, many styles did in fact exist simultaneously in the late eighteenth and early nineteenth century.

Nor was it absolutely necessary that Neoclassicism and Romanticism should have come into being when they did. However, the sequence of developments in art in England and France over a century shows that the occurrence of the styles was not random and that their correlations with extra-artistic phenomena were more than coincidental. Although changes in key aspects of imagery and form had a corresponding development in both countries, the styles matured about a quarter of a century later in France. And these developments corresponded to a lag of the same interval in the social texture of the societies.

At a given time, an intertwining of cultural elements and values, though independent in origin, makes for conflicts and tensions: thus laws dating from the Middle Ages are still operative, untouched in form or substance by modern jurisprudence. This makes possible a certain independence within the interdependence, preventing an absolute determinism and making possible a certain transcendence of the immediate.

An undifferentiated long-range view, however, may be as misleading as cultural myopia. For instance, even though Neoclassicism and Romanticism came into being during the emergence of the newer ideas about art, the artist, and individuality, they were not different aspects of the same development. They were formed of various elements stemming from the Renaissance, which in itself contained different and even contradictory possibilities of selection in art and in life.

Once in existence, a new style does not displace and obliterate older styles. Just as there are anticipatory marginal features in art, so also are there residual elements or survivals, such as Ingresque Neoclassicism, and the persistence of older themes and practices in even the more advanced examples of Romantic painting. In addition, many of the psychological and intellectual elements associated with them, as well as purely artistic features, had been current at least since the fifteenth century; with Romanticism, some may even extend back to Celtic times.

Of course, all styles more or less reconcile conflicting tendencies, but forms of reconciliation vary. As the ideas, values, and feelings associated with the term "romantic" became more dominant in general perception and in art, they coalesced with attitudes toward the artist and the individual human being to form a system. Romantic *elements* became the *style* of Romanticism. A new style was formed in the clustering of developments from several realms, and could only have occurred in its peculiar form at that time.

Without reference to particular situations in art and in society, facile matchings are misleading. Early Christian art, for example, was actually the contemporary pagan art of Imperial Rome. Similarly, the dramatic political events of the late eighteenth and early nineteenth century did not cause the formation of the art. The styles in France actually preceded the revolutions in which their artists were participants or witnesses, while in England there was no political revolution at all.

In one of those retrogressive effects that plague revolutions, the French Revolution actually delayed the growth of Romantic painting in France. Its leaders selected Neoclassicism as its style from among others that were current, including a proto-Romantic art. But without the profound social upheaval of which the Revolution was a violent symptom, the genesis and character of both styles would have been different.

While the styles emerged from the art tradition, their realization was intimately molded by this broader ideological, emotional, and economic basis. For the function and status of art and artist changed in the new social structure that resulted from the gradual rise to prominence and power of the middle class, which also affected the attitudes, ideas, and interests entering, through artists, into art.

However, neither Neoclassicism nor Romanticism was the art of the middle class. Each style, and art in general, had a different relationship to the middle class and to different sectors of the middle class in each country, as did individual artists, irrespective of style or country. For the more complex and fluid the society, the less attached to, or expressive of, specific groups are styles in art or in life.

Though the new institutional and class ties of artists did not rigidly determine the kind of art produced, they did have a directive and sometimes a decisive effect in creating publics, on whom even the most independent artist is, in some measure, dependent. At the same time, the spread of ideas of the worth of the ordinary individual led to greater stress both on the artist's revelation of himself and on the participation of the spectator in the work of art—which conflicted with the idea of the autonomy of the artist. From the complex interplay between artist and public, there resulted new expectations of what art and artists should be, in the light of new elaborations upon old legends of the artist.

One of the myths stemming from the Romantic tradition is that an artist paints what he feels and that therefore art is self-expression— a reversal of the much older and equally mistaken assumption that an artist paints what he sees. But even ordinary perception is not simple; as experimental and psychoanalytic psychology have shown, it occurs in the light of many basic moods and attitudes. The kind of vision involved in artistic creation is even more complex, for the artist sees not only as an ordinary individual, but also in terms of elaborations of perception that are stylized—that is, given form—through the materials and problems of a specialized activity which, moreover, has a history of its own.

The myth of self-expression also involves ideas about the personality of the artist and its connections with his work. Actually, the personal element is not necessarily the most important one in the formation of group styles. Although it is difficult to imagine the particular character of Neoclassicism and Romanticism without David, Constable and Delacroix, the general form of the styles would have developed regardless of the existence of these masters, for others were painting in the group styles before their works became models to follow.

At any rate, a certain type of personality cannot simply be deduced from a certain type of art style; both Delacroix and David suffered from compulsiveness but evolved very different styles. And if an art style necessarily reflected personality, one might suppose that an artist who simultaneously practices different styles does not have a well-integrated personality; but Corot seems to have been among the best-balanced of men. Moreover, even outstanding artists like Fragonard, Corot, Turner, and Constable may execute paintings that seem antithetic to the "personality" for the purpose of making money or of winning recognition. The relationship of an artist's inner and outer life to what he creates is expressed in many different ways and is not revealed by his art without consideration of its place among other works and trends of the time.

Nor does art reflect the world. Viewed as mirrors of a prevailing mood, Romanticism and Neoclassicism seem to be trick mirrors and even reverse images of their times. If an art style reflected its epoch, French Neoclassicism would be the product of a quiet, well-ordered world, and Romanticism, of social and political turbulence. Actually, both styles incubated and grew in times of drastic social change.

The semiautonomous development of art styles within the internal history of art makes it impossible for a work of art to be a direct revelation of the society in which it was made. For all elements in a given work are not "expressive" of contemporary concerns but may be disguises for them, or vestiges of older ideas that have lost all specific significance and have persisted through inertia. Art may express what a powerful extraneous interest wants to inculcate, rather than what actually exists, as was the case of the official art program in mid-eighteenth century France. Even propagandistic art is not a revelation of the type of government that commissioned it. The forms and symbols may belong to different realms, as we can see in the classicism of the pre-Revolutionary and Revolutionary David, and later in the pretentious classicistic monuments of nineteenth- and twentieth-century states, democratic as well as totalitarian.

Correlative with the myths of art as self-expression and art as a mirror of the times is the myth of artists as prophets and art as a forecast of things to come, in society as well as in art. Actually, since before they are artists they are men, the psychological disposition of painters and other social factors preceded the art styles that seem most closely connected with them. The complex of factors was already operative in various aspects of English society considerably before Romantic painting came into being. In France, ideas and attitudes were already operative in the mid-eighteenth century which later resulted in the artistic and political revolutions. Even the occurrence of marginal features is not a reliable forecast of more widespread changes in the specific area of painting or in the attitudes in the outer world with which they seem to have much in common, for one does not know if or when they will recur.

And even when these features emerge on a broader scale, their combination into a style probably will not, as a totality, have a counterpart outside art.

The prophetic illusion occurs because art often makes graphically visible what people may passively or unconsciously accept or practice in real life, and because they confuse social and art images. The general inertia of the image often leads persons who may be advanced in many of their ideas to prefer older forms and imagery in the essentially separate world of art.

Like other human activities, such as making love, eating, and physiological functions that have no immediately relevant connection with other social activities, art also leads a more or less autonomous existence in the lives of individuals, including its creators, and in the social system. But though art is only semiautonomous in society, it does have the autonomous function of evoking affective responses. This makes it an essentially ambiguous medium of expression, for it is created by the artist and experienced by the spectator through a network of strands from the art tradition and from attitudes, ideas, and values that are not necessarily aesthetic in origin.

In its ambiguity, it is typical of human behavior. As William James wrote in 1880, "Societies of men are just like individuals, in that both at any given moment offer ambiguous potentialities of development."[1] More recent theory and evidence from experimental psychology, psychiatry, and sociology have shown the equivocal nature of relationships to be a basic characteristic of man's existence.[2] Indeed, art is of continual interest and value from the very ambiguity of its relationships, which makes it a source of stimulation and wonder.

In essence art is not really communication, for it evokes ideas and responses that may not necessarily correspond to those of the artist in creating the work. Even representational art that conveys specific information through legible subject matter has different affects in different styles. Of course, intense aesthetic experience involves a sense of rapport or union, but not, as in love, with the psyche or feelings of another person. It is therefore extrapersonal and somewhat detached from other areas of experience, making for the factor of aesthetic distance which has often been remarked upon by aestheticians. This sense of union (or unification or form), which is experienced by appreciators as well as by creators, is often mistaken for communion with the artist or with ideas or feelings transmitted by him.[3]

Though the painter or his painting do not necessarily communicate messages, as these are generally conceived, the impact of the work of art nevertheless must rest on something which it contains or which the spectator sees or "projects" upon it. Otherwise it would have no meaning, even in an affective sense. The very opposition of the detractors of a certain style shows that there is something in it they are reacting against.

The flourishing of a group style and its survival show a deep affectiveness for a public. Even if an artist hits upon a new and original idea or technique, he cannot exploit it fully without a circle or public of appreciators who—because of the practical exigencies of creativity as well as of physical existence—are preferably also purchasers. Although art is semiautonomous, the experiencing as well as the creation of art involves extra-artistic ideas of artists and the moods and attitudes of a public.

Because of the varied backgrounds, attitudes, and interests in a complex and dynamic society, all making up a heterogeneity and overlapping of tastes, the psychological meanings of a particular style may vary for different artists and for different members of the public. The course of development of styles over a period of time shows that they served different psychological functions and even had different meanings attached to familiar thematic signs or symbols at different times. Therefore the descriptive value of "romanticism" and "classicism" is vitiated by their use to explain categories of problems which have no existence outside the dialectics created by the terms themselves. Perhaps their continued use in this fashion bespeaks a sense of order gained from sweeping classifications, no matter how misleading or fallacious, of complex phenomena.

The matching of qualities may be deceptive, as we have seen with the different meanings of "free," which may apply differently to the art and to the social behavior of individuals. Although there seems to be evidence for the compensatory role of art, at least in the late eighteenth and early nineteenth centuries, it is subject to qualifications. Stormier

activity among artists existed in a milieu, France, that was not so discouraging for art as in England—a process reminiscent of the occurrence
of revolutions at times of reformism rather than greater suppressiveness.
In England where there was less opportunity in life for emotional ex-
ternalization, the paintings of individual Romantics were more "free"
than in France. And the earlier British portrayal of suffering and
criminality, which was not for a select audience and was even more
prevalent in popular imagery, seems due to a craving for the destructive
rebel in a society that increasingly repressed open emotional expression.
Similarly, the emergence of a Romantic style during the Bourbon Restoration might be interpreted as the expression of a yearning for libertarian
forces during an era of suppressiveness, compensating for what was
missing in life.

This seems evidence for what is often said to be the cathartic element
of art, which has been used in characterizations of art as unfettered self-
expression. Davidian art apparently contradicts both these points. However, in catharsis as it operated in a highly formalized way among the
Greeks, the element of control as well as discharge was important. It
gives the artist and the spectator a feeling not only of release (which can
be achieved in other ways than through art) but also of the control
which gives a feeling of mastery. Proportioning of discharge and control
varies, and makes for a restrictive or a more emotionalized style. The
historical development of styles shows that one aspect may be dominant
at a particular time or that two or more may coexist so that strong
distinctions may not even be made between styles by the artists themselves, unless—as occurred between Ingres and Delacroix—a volatile
atmosphere created by partisans forms an irritating and provocative situation which may lead to the assumption of opposing positions.

Furthermore, the persistence of old subjects and techniques in some
of the advanced French Romantic art was due not so much to repression
and compensation (which after all are constant mechanisms in the human
psyche), but to the supporting effect of the art tradition. For though
transcendence is kept within bounds by limiting factors of the milieu,
the relative beneficence of a milieu may itself impose limitations. On the
other hand, the inhospitable soil of England nourished the most advanced
Romantic painting in the art of Constable. Beginning with some of the
Romantics and Neoclassicists in the 1830s, art in France also developed
away from the official apparatus which traditionally had sustained it, de-

pending instead on newer supports, which artists were able to find in a supposedly materialistic society.

However important "innate" talents may be, their realization depends largely upon their valuation by the society. Let us speculate as to what our artists' styles would have been if they had lived in other settings. The more impetuous tendencies in David might have been expressed more freely if he had been born toward the end of the eighteenth century rather than just before its halfway point. This view is encouraged by his changing and heterogeneous styles. He might have painted in a coloristic and activated style, as the Romantics did. Ingres, if born earlier in the eighteenth century, might have been happy as a Rococo painter under the protection of a noble patron, without feeling threatened on all sides. The unstable conditions of the early nineteenth century seem to have encouraged the development of feelings of persecution which were present early in his life: he was already at war with imaginary enemies while Delacroix was still a child. But if Ingres had lived in England where he might not have had his feelings of insecurity assuaged by success, he might have shared Haydon's fate. If Ary Scheffer had lived in England, would he perhaps not have been an artist at all? Might not his thirst for action have led him to become a Protestant evangelist or a colonial adventurer? And would a man of superior literary and speculative abilities like Delacroix have been a professional painter at all in the twentieth century, or would he have found painting satisfying only as an avocation, in conjunction with a more purely intellectual profession?

Our contemporaries still pursue ideals in art and in life which the Romantics affirmed but failed to realize completely. Since the time of the Romantics an even greater value has been placed on "freedom" for itself alone and for "unfettered" expression of emotions and impulses —ideas which grew with the loosening of institutional ties. In older art also, the affective features of formal elements gave styles a psychological function which was sometimes independent of thematic content. Actually, many French Romantic and Neoclassical paintings have the same subject matter but fully realized French Romantic figure pieces have a closer affective kinship with English Romantic landscapes than with French Neoclassical works.

In much twentieth-century art, these basic impulses seem exposed in a cultivation of impulsiveness, often with the rationale of misapplied psychoanalytic ideas. Even in willfully automatic painting, inventions almost immediately become conventions that mediate to prevent direct transcription of primary processes. It became the program of many abstract expressionists to try to transcribe these elements and basic body-psychical processes in the "direct" action of fastening paints and other materials to a flat surface. Sometimes their nonobjective art is curiously realistic, disdaining to suggest open or empty space through illusionistic devices or techniques and actually creating empty spaces by punching holes through the canvas. It is therefore simultaneously a more "natural" and a more artificial art, yet another variation on the old principle that art, to use the words of Delacroix, "lives through fictions." [4]

With art's almost complete separation from its former uses and the widespread rejection of realistic preoccupations, the "fictions" have drawn farther away from the articulateness of literary frames of reference and closer to the suggestiveness or abstractions of music, which Kandinsky and others thought the abstract elements of painting could approximate.

The aspect of modern art, in its impetuous and its highly intellectual-ized forms, which remains most disturbing to the general public is its disdain for the touchstone of "natural" appearances as the main concern of art. For people are still accustomed to think of images in art in terms of the beautiful, benevolent ghost of the Renaissance tradition. Curiously, while most people still reject or are bewildered by modern painting and sculpture, they have accepted modern art when embodied in the design of automobiles, furniture, appliances, fabrics, and houses. But many who accept the forms of modern art in a materially utilitarian context do not find them acceptable in painting, since the imagery and forms do not fulfill their expectations of what art should be. Possibly as he becomes accustomed to formerly hidden aspects of matter and the universe through the electronmicroscope, giant telescopes, and air and space travel, the man in the street will also take as a matter of course the abstract images in art. At any rate, the vagueness of specific meanings and the stress on affect and impulse of much abstract art at once act as bridge and barrier between the artist and his public.

Modern art may be for the many at the same time that it is for the few. For in an open society, the possibility exists that a mass audience can be an elite, or that an elite can be so large that it will constitute something of a mass audience. In a relatively fluid and prosperous society, members of elite groups are not the chosen few; they choose themselves since even a person of humble origin can, with application or luck, join their ranks.

For since the Romantics the process of social democratization has gone much farther, breeding new expectations and disappointments. More members of the public are freer than ever to be discontented with some of the very features of society that enabled them to attain their affluent state, and have more leisure time to fill with more meaningful activities; for many of them modern art and artists seem models of deviance and creativity. Unlike others who depart from the standards or activities of everyday life, such as juvenile delinquents and dope addicts, the artist is a "good deviant" whose life and work make him an idealized prototype of Alienated Man. The sharply visible difference between abstract art and Western art of the past has accentuated the old image of the artist as a rebel, independent of and scornful of the world. Actually, painters are not totally contemptuous of contemporary culture. Many derive inspiration from science and technology, and may make odd attempts to justify their practice in terms of the fourth dimension.

The artist's intense commitment to a precarious occupation seems a counterbalance to the leveling of aspirations in the society of the Organization Man; he is regarded as one of the few who uphold values that others profess but negate in their work. Despite economic embarrassment, the artist seems to wield unpurchasable power as he manipulates an environment in the world of his painting. Because of his archetypal sacred aspect, the hope of salvation is attached to him in a world that badly needs saving. His admirers place an unfair burden upon the artist by expecting him to accomplish through art the inner and outer metamorphoses that belong to other spheres of life. At the same time, the wider dissemination of the idea that every man is potentially an artist implies that every man can participate in these metamorphoses. The probable failure of such expectations may sow the seeds of disillusionment from which the artist himself and the idea of art must inevitably suffer.

Since painting today functions largely as an archetype of value, it has acquired the standing of a social or spiritual fetish, reminiscent of objects having a specific magical or supernatural property in primitive societies. This has increasingly become true as older forms of such attachments have withered and died in our culture. Those social fetishes we do recognize, such as automobiles, refrigerators, and jewelry, have only the ephemeral value of economic or social status, without the more permanent qualities and deeper connotations of the true fetish or spiritual emblem. Art is one of the few elements in our society that can give the spectator as well as the artist a sense of transcendence.

While closer to everyday institutions that offer a more reliable livelihood, commercial art, which often requires a high degree of technical competence, is split off from what is considered to be "Art"—to which the scribbles and daubs of children seem closer. For though over a period of time the forms of commercial art approximate those of Art, they are considered to be incompatible because they serve different purposes. Commercial art is really "useful" in the institutions and transactions of the everyday world. But fine art pretends to be faithful, as commercial art does not, to highly esteemed basic human impulses and feelings and certain assumed values without manipulating them for the extraneous end of selling cigarettes or deodorants. Much of the support for today's fine art is emblematic of a feeling of the inadequacy of other cultural products and institutions to embody those values. On the other hand, a desire to find worth in today's life through its characteristic appurtenances probably lies behind the vogue for "pop" and "junk" art, with their resignation to or glorification of mass culture.

Under such circumstances, is great art possible? To a large extent, our ideas of greatness in art and artists are conditioned by Greek, medieval, and Renaissance art. Perhaps the older art seems on a higher level or more complete because of a greater continuity between social and religious institutions and the lives of individuals, resulting in a higher degree of shared, specific meanings in realms that seem superior to daily life.

The more fully people are persuaded of the worth of art as a carrier of value, the more they are willing to suspend an uneasiness about equivocal meanings which seem to incorporate highly esteemed human attributes. Those qualities of individuality—originality, spontaneity, and naïveté, which were more prominent in the theory than in the practice of Romantic painters—are assiduously cultivated today. Respect for these qualities is strengthened by our high valuation of the child's art work as we long nostalgically for a carefree, comfortably dependent, and more optimistic phase of life. The permissiveness accorded the acts of children no doubt accounts in part for the vogue for abstract expressionism. The taste for the delightful art of children, however, has fostered a misunderstanding about the nature of spontaneity in adult art. For the child after the age of six does not reject his earlier "free" creations simply through corruption by academic or "traditional" instruction, but, rather, through his desire to master objects in the real world as he grows up and matures emotionally and intellectually.

The mature artist, in painting abstractly, is following a new tradition, beginning in the late eighteenth and early nineteenth centuries, that respects characteristics identified with, but not identical with, those of children. The high regard for analogous features in modern art has helped submerge esteem for the intellectual qualities of great artists, a respect which had accorded them high status in the Renaissance and had persisted in the time of the outstanding Romantics.

The lack of definite standards seems compatible with the indeterminate goals and means of art. This indeterminacy is given greater intellectual respectability by the new prestige of science, which also deals with intangibles and abstractions. The artist must suffer from the setting of an artificial chasm, however modish, between the rational and the emotional, whose union makes us specifically human and art a higher form of activity. For as his skills and the content of his work have become less accessible in terms of communicable speech and knowledge, he is removed from the terms of reference of a profession, while at the same time he is bound to the status of a professional in terms of expectations. There is often a thin dividing line between the art work of the professional and the amateur.

Actually, it is difficult to criticize a great deal of modern painting in a convincing and demonstrable way because of its equivocal meanings. Since early detractors of modern art turned its ambiguity as a weapon against it, a habit of militant defensiveness grew which persists in the taste-making apparatus of universities, museums, and periodicals all sponsoring a cause that battled for its life, sustained by only a few devoted adherents, half a century ago.

The ambiguities of the imagery and forms in modern art and of the image of the artist reinforce one another. Although modern art has passed its "revolutionary" phase, there is a reluctance among intellectuals, who feel a kinship with the artist at least in his relative social estrangement, to criticize his work adversely. The difficulty the artist has with material existence poses a strong moral question for those who, by their criticisms, might endanger his livelihood. For his importance seems to transcend the individual in a world where cherished values are in doubt or at stake and where painting is a highly expendable commodity. The artist's sincerity, above all, is not to be questioned. Thus his vulnerability actually performs the service of exempting him from some of the reproaches to which other men are subject. In struggling to maintain his identity, his status, and his self-respect in a society where businessmen, lawyers, physicians, clergymen, and scientists have well established roles in the main pursuits of the community, that marginal man, the artist, is trapped by his own myths. In his rootless freedom, he often feels constrained to enact the stereotype of "the artist" in rationalization of his precarious situation. At the same time, he benefits from the myths which, cherished by the public as an ideal image, make it possible for him still to exist in a semiautonomous sense.

But since modern art's symbolic relevance overrides its objectively functional irrelevance, the symbols the painter creates must be adequate to sustain the high value his public accords his work. Although it is hard to specify standards, dodging the issue of quality and worth in an emblem of value can only create the danger that the images of art and artist may become a mirage. There is of course no easy solution for the problems in creating and appreciating art that have been aggravated by its symbolically elevated and socially displaced position. Yet neither artists nor public need passively regard the situation as a neutralizing dilemma. They can accept it as a challenge to the psychological and spiritual activity involved in art, a vital element of an intellectually and emotionally affluent life.

Chronology of Artists

FRANCE		ENGLAND	
Antoine Watteau	1684-1721	William Hogarth	1697-1764
Jean-Baptiste Siméon		Richard Wilson	1714-1782
Chardin	1699-1779	Joshua Reynolds	1723-1792
François Boucher	1703-1770	Gavin Hamilton	1723-1798
Joseph Vernet	1712-1789	George Stubbs	1724-1806
Joseph Marie Vien	1716-1809	Thomas Gainsborough	1727-1788
Jean Honoré Fragonard	1732-1806	Joseph Wright (Wright of	
Hubert Robert	1733-1808	Derby)	1734-1797
François Guillaume		John Singleton Copley	1737-1815
Ménageot	1744-1816	Benjamin West	1738-1820
François André Vincent	1746-1816	James Barry	1741-1806
Jacques Louis David	1748-1825	Henry Fuseli	1741-1825
Marie Ann Elisabeth		John Flaxman	1755-1826
Vigée-Lebrun	1755-1842	William Blake	1757-1827
Pierre Paul Prud'hon	1758-1823	John Opie	1761-1807
Anne Louis Girodet		Thomas Lawrence	1769-1830
Trioson	1767-1824	Thomas Girtin	1775-1802
François Gérard	1770-1837	Joseph William Mallord	
Antoine-Jean Gros	1771-1835	Turner	1775-1851
Pierre Narcisse Guérin	1774-1833	John Constable	1776-1837
François Marius Granet	1775-1849	David Wilkie	1785-1841
Jean Auguste Dominique		Benjamin Haydon	1786-1846
Ingres	1780-1867	William Etty	1787-1849
Horace Vernet	1789-1863	John Martin	1789-1854
Théodore Géricault	1791-1824	Richard Parkes Bonington	1802-1828
Ary Scheffer	1795-1858	Edwin Henry Landseer	1802-1873
Camille Corot	1796-1875		
Eugène Devéria	1797-1856		
Paul Delaroche	1797-1856		
Eugène Delacroix	1798-1863		
Tony Johannot	1803-1852		
Alexandre Decamps	1803-1860		
Paul Huet	1803-1869		
Louis Boulanger	1807-1867		
Honoré Daumier	1808-1879		
Paul-Joseph Chenavard	1808-1895		
Hippolyte Flandrin	1809-1864		
Théodore Rousseau	1812-1867		
Thomas Couture	1815-1879		
Ernest Meissonier	1815-1891		
Théodore Chassériau	1819-1856		
Adolphe Bouguereau	1825-1905		

Notes

ONE

1. For the "physiognomic fallacy" in the history of art, see E. H. Gombrich, "On Physiognomic Perception," *Daedalus,* Winter, 1960, pp. 222-41.

2. See, for instance, Hans Sedlmayr, *Art in Crisis,* tr. by Brian Battershaw (London: Hollis and Carter, 1957), pp. 5, 177.

3. See particularly Rudolf Arnheim, *Art and Visual Perception* (Berkeley and Los Angeles: University of California Press, 1957).

4. For these and other theories, see Meyer Schapiro, "Style," *Anthropology Today,* prepared under the chairmanship of A. L. Kroeber (Chicago: The University of Chicago Press, 1953).

5. Herbert Read, *A Concise History of Modern Painting* (London: Thames and Hudson, 1959), p. 50.

6. For criticisms of these writings, see Richard Wollheim, "Sociological Explanation of the Arts: Some Distinctions," *Proceedings of the Third International Congress on Aesthetics* (Turin, Italy, 1957), pp. 404-10; E. H. Gombrich, Review of Arnold Hauser's "Social History of Art," *Art Bulletin,* XXXV, March 1953, pp. 79-84.

7. Arnold Hauser, *The Social History of Art* (2 vols.; New York: Alfred A. Knopf, 1951), vol. II, pp. 530-34.

8. Frederick Antal, "Reflections on Classicism and Romanticism," *The Burlington Magazine,* 66, April 1935, pp. 159-68.

9. "Toward a Theory of Creativity," *Etc.,* XI, summer 1954, pp. 249-60.

10. Bernice T. Eiduson, "Artist and Nonartist: a Comparative Study," *Journal of Personality,* 26, March 1958, pp. 13-28.

11. Twenty-third Lecture, *Introductory Lectures.*

TWO

1. E. J. Delécluze, *Journal,* 1824-28, ed. by Robert Baschet (Paris: Editions Bernard Grasset, 1948), pp. 213-14.

2. *Ibid.,* pp. 213-14.

3. Francis D. Klingender, *Art and the Social Revolution* (London: Noel Carrington, 1947), pp. 39-55; Alfred de Foville, *La Transformation des moyens de transport et ses conséquences économiques et sociales* (Paris: Librairie Guillaumin et Cie., 1880), pp. 5-20.

4. Michel Florisoone, "Constable and the 'Massacres de Scio' by Delacroix," *Journal of the Warburg and Courtauld Institutes,* 20, 1957, pp. 180-85.

5. Léon Rosenthal, *Du Romantisme au réalisme* (Paris: Librairie Renouard, 1914), pp. 165-71.

6. C. R. Leslie, *Memoirs of the Life of John Constable* (London: Phaidon Press, Ltd., 1951), p. 95.

7. From an issue of 1824. S. Charléty, *La Restauration,* vol. IV, in Ernest Lavisse, *Histoire de France Contemporaine* (Paris: Librairie Hachette, 1921), p. 214.

8. *Ibid.*

9. "On the Discrimination of Romanticisms," *Essays in the History of Ideas* (Baltimore: The Johns Hopkins Press, 1948), reprinted from *Publications of the Modern Language Association,* XXXIX, 1924, pp. 229-53.

10. T. E. Hulme, *Speculations: Essays on Humanism and the Philosophy of Art,* H. Read, ed. (2nd ed.; London, 1954), pp. 116, 255-56; Gregory Zilboorg, *A History of Medical Psychology* (New York: W. W. Norton and Co., 1941), pp. 190, 498; Alex Comfort, *Art and Social Responsibility* (London: The Falcon Press Ltd., 1946), p. 18; Otto Rank, *Art and Artist,* tr. by Charles Francis Atkinson (New York: Alfred A. Knopf, 1932), pp. 418-24.

11. Benjamin Robert Haydon, *Autobiography and Memoirs, 1786-1846,* ed. from his journals by Tom Taylor (2 vols.; London: Peter Davies, 1926), vol. I, p. 147.

12. Leslie, p. 199.

13. George Sand, *Histoire de ma vie* (4 vols.; Paris: Calmann-Lévy, Editeurs, 1928), vol. IV, pp. 159-60.

14. Franz Liszt, *Pages romantiques* (Paris: Librairie Félix Alcan, 1912), p. 121. See H. A. Needham, *Le Développement de l'esthétique sociologique en France et en Angleterre au XIX*ᵉ *siècle* (Paris: Ancienne Honoré Champion, 1926), p. 147; Jean-G. Lossier, *Le Rôle social de l'art selon Proudhon* (Paris: Librairie Philosophique J. Vrin, 1937); Marguerite Thibert, *Le Rôle social de l'art d'après les Saint-Simoniens* (Paris: Librairie des Sciences Economiques et Sociales).

15. Liszt, p. 4.

16. Planned in 1848, these murals were never executed because of the resurgence of ecclesiastical authority under Napoleon III. See Joseph Buche, *L'Ecole mystique de Lyons, 1776-1844* (Librairie Félix Alcan, 1935), p. 262; Théophile Silvestre, *Les Artistes français* (2 vols.; Paris: Les Editions G. Crès et Cie., 1926), vol. II, p. 117.

17. For this development, see especially Paul Oskar Kristeller, "The Modern System of the Arts: a Study in the History of Aesthetics," *Journal of the History of Ideas,* 12, October 1951, pp. 496-527; 13, January 1952, pp. 17-46. See also Ernst Kris, "The Image of the Artist," in *Psychoanalytic Explorations in Art* (New York: International Universities Press, Inc., 1952), pp. 64-87; Georges Matoré, "Les Notions de l'art et d'artiste à l'époque romantique," *Revue des Sciences Humaines,* 1951, pp. 120-36; E. H. Gombrich, "The Renaissance Concept of Artistic Progress and Its Consequences," Acts of the 17th International Congress for the History of Art, Amsterdam, 1952, Imprimerie Nationale des Pays-Bas, La Haye, 1955, pp. 291-307.

18. In Lessing's *Laocoön,* according to E. H. Gombrich, "Lessing (Lecture on a Master Mind)," *Proceedings of the British Academy,* 1957, pp. 133-56.

19. Haydon, vol. I, p. 103.

20. Mona Wilson, *The Life of William Blake* (New York: Oxford University Press, 1949), p. 374.

THREE

1. The increase was from 354 to 2,159 between 1789 and 1838, and from 509 in 1810 to 1,375 in 1830. Thus the number of painters rose by 456 during the first twenty-year period, by 866 during the second period, and by 784 during the next eight years. See Rosenthal, *Du Romantisme au réalisme,* p. 77. For demography, see Alexander Morris Carr-Saunders, *Population* (London: Oxford University Press, 1925).

2. Jean Locquin, *La Peinture d'histoire en France de 1747 à 1785* (Paris: Henri Laurens, Editeur, 1912), p. 52.

3. Heinrich Heine, *The Salon,* tr. by Charles Godfrey Leland (London: William Heinemann, 1893), pp. 61-62.

4. This art resembled that of the Nazarenes, a group of German painters. See Buche.

5. See Alexis de Tocqueville, *The Old Regime and the French Revolution,* tr. by Stuart Gilbert (New York: Doubleday Anchor Books, 1955); G. M. Trevelyan, *English Social History* (New York: Longmans, Green and Co., 1943).

6. Kristeller.

7. Locquin; Nikolaus Pevsner, *Academies of Art, Past and Present* (Cambridge: University Press, 1940).

8. Locquin, pp. 153-57, 196, 216-17.

9. Pevsner; Ellis K. Waterhouse, "English Painting and France in the Eighteenth Century," *Journal of the Warburg Institute,* 15, 1952, pp. 122-35.

10. William T. Whitley, *Art in England,* 1821-1837 (Cambridge: University Press, 1930), p. 198.

11. Haydon, vol. I, p. 31.

12. William T. Whitley, *Art in England,* 1800-1820 (Cambridge: University Press, 1928), p. 297.

13. A. P. Oppé, "Art," chapter X, *Early Victorian England,* ed. by G. M. Young (London: Oxford University Press, 1934), p. 109.

14. Frederick Antal, *Hogarth and His Place in European Art* (London: Routledge & Kegan Paul, 1962), p. 13.

15. Locquin, p. 48; Pevsner, p. 191.

16. David L. Dowd, *Pageant-Master of the Republic,* The University of Nebraska Studies, June, 1948, p. 23.

17. Whitley, 1800-1820, p. 75; Delécluze, *Journal,* p. 295; Rosenthal, *Du Romantisme au réalisme,* p. 50; Louis Véron, *Memoirs d'un bourgeois de Paris* (5 vols.; Paris: Librairie Nouvelle, 1856), vol. I, p. 26; Paul Hazard, "Il y a cent ans," *Revue des Deux Mondes,* 20 octobre 1935, pp. 892-905.

18. Rudolph Wittkower, *Born Under Saturn. The Character and Conduct of Artists: A Documented History from Antiquity to the French Revolution* (London: Weidenfeld and Nicolson, 1963), pp. 18-20.

19. Whitley, 1800-1820, p. 315.

20. E. J. Delécluze, *Louis-David, son école et son temps* (Paris: Didier, Librairie-Editeur, 1855), p. 212.

21. These artists were Trimolet, Steinheil, Meissonier, Daubigny, Dechaumes. See Rosenthal, *Du Romantisme au réalisme,* p. 30.

22. Thomas Ashcroft, *English Art and English Society* (London: Peter Davies, Ltd., 1936), p. 36.

23. Mme. Marie Louise Elisabeth Vigée-Lebrun, *Mémoirs,* tr. by Lionel Strachey (New York: Doubleday & Co., 1907), p. 185.

24. Mona Wilson, p. 147.

25. Rosenthal, *Du Romantisme au réalisme, pp.* 158-65. See also Léonce Bénédite *Théodore Chassériau, sa vie et son oeuvre* (Paris: Braun, 1931).

26. Amaury Duval, *L'Atelier d'Ingres* (Paris: Les Editions G. Crès et Cie., 1924), p. 229.

27. Ada Earland, *John Opie and His Circle* (London: Hutchinson and Co., 1911), p. 195.

28. Lawrence painted this picture between 1796 and 1804. See George Somes Layard, *Sir Thomas Lawrence's Letter-Bag* (New York: Longmans, Green and Co., 1906), p. 225.

29. Pevsner, p. 35.

30. Delécluze, *Journal,* p. 295.

31. *Géricault raconté par lui-même et par ses amis* (Vésenaz-Génève: Pierre Cailler, Editeur, 1947), pp. 79ff.

32. Théophile Silvestre, *Les Artistes français* (2 vols.; Paris: Les Editions G. Crès et Cie., 1926). vol. I, pp. 208ff; Léon Séché, *Le Cénacle de Joseph Delorme,* 1827-1830 (Paris: Mercure de France, 1925), p. 100.

33. Raymond Escholier, *Gros, ses amis et ses élèves* (Paris: Librairie Floury, 1936).

34. Whitley, 1800-1820, pp. 50-51; 1821-1837, p. 291.

35. Oppé, p. 122n.

36. Véron, vol. I, p. 275.

37. M. Sturge Henderson, *Constable* (London: Duckworth and Co., 1905), p. 42.

38. Cunningham, quoted by Arthur Symons, *William Blake* (New York: E. P. Dutton and Co., 1907), pp. 420ff.

39. *Ingres raconté par lui-même et par ses amis* (Vésenaz-Génève: Pierre Cailler, Editeur, 1947), pp. 35.

40. Liszt, p. 12.

41. Séché, vol. II, p. 128.

42. Rosenthal, *Du Romantisme au réalisme;* Théophile Gautier, *Histoire du romantisme* (3° édition; Paris: G. Charpentier, Editeur, 1877, first published 1874).

43. *Ingres raconté,* p. 175.

44. *Journal,* tr. by Walter Pach (New York: Crown Publishers, 1948), April 24, 1824, p. 73.

45. *Du Romantisme au réalisme,* p. 176n.

46. W. G. Constable, *John Flaxman* (London: University of London Press, Ltd., 1927), p. 46.

47. *Journal,* February 19, 1850, p. 210.

48. Duval.

49. *Journal,* November 25, 1860, p. 689, May 15 and June 1, 1855, pp. 462, 464-65. In keeping with the exaggerated stories of antagonism between the two men, Delacroix's remarks of June 1 are often omitted from writings about these artists; see, for instance, Agnes Mongan, "Ingres and the Antique," *Journal of the Warburg Institute,* 10, 1947, pp. 1-13.

50. Whitley, 1800-1820, p. 106.

51. Gautier, pp. 220ff.

52. See Louise Rosenblatt, *L'Idée de l'art pour l'art dans la littérature anglaise pendant la période Victorienne* (Paris: Librairie Ancienne Honoré Champion, 1931).

53. Robert K. Merton, "Science and Economy of Seventeenth Century England," chapter XIX in *Social Theory and Social Structure* (revised; Glencoe, Illinois: The Free Press, 1957), pp. 607-627.

54. Regarding hatred of the bourgeois, see Albert Cassagne, *La Théorie de l'art pour l'art en France* (Paris: L. Dorbon, 1959, first published 1906).

55. Haydon, vol. I, pp. 138-39.

56. Frances Trollope, *Paris and the Parisians in 1835* (New York: Harper and Bros., 1836), p. 192.

57. Rosenthal, *Du Romantisme au réalisme,* p. 23.

58. *Journal,* January 16, 1860, p. 655. See also January 13, 1851, pp. 540-41.

59. Locquin, pp. 25, 33.

60. In the Palais Bourbon: the Salon du Roi (1833-37) and the ceiling of the library of the Chamber of Deputies (1838-47); in the Luxembourg Palace, the ceiling of the library (1841-46).

61. Rosenthal, *Du Romantisme au réalisme,* p. 10.

62. Henry Lytton Bulwer, *The Monarchy of the Middle Classes* (London: Richard Bentley, 1836), pp. 74ff. See also R. H. Gretton, *The English Middle Classes* (London: G. Bell and Sons, Ltd., 1919).

63. Waterhouse; Oppé, p. 115.

64. See Elie Halévy, *England in 1815,* tr. by E. I. Watkins and D. A. Baker (London: Ernest Benn, Ltd., 1949).

65. Oppé, p. 122n.

66. Mona Wilson, p. 5.

67. Lord Ronald Charles Sutherland Gower, *Sir David Wilkie* (London: George Bell and Sons, 1902), p. 6.

68. Oppé, pp. 493-94; Whitley, 1821-1837, p. 198.

FOUR

1. Whitley, 1800-1820, p. 302.

2. Gower, p. 26.

3. Henderson, p. 153.

4. Gower, p. 60.

5. See Kristeller.

6. *Ibid.* See also E. H. Gombrich, "The Renaissance Concept of Artistic Progress and Its Consequences"; "Visual Metaphors of Value in Art," *Symbols and Values: An Initial Study,* Third Symposium on Science, Philosophy and Religion, ed. by L. Bryson and others (New York: Harper and Bros., 1954); *Art and Illusion* (New York: Pantheon Books, 1960), p. 155.

7. Brewster Rogerson, "The Art of Painting the Passions," *Journal of the History of Ideas,* XIV, January 1953, pp. 68-94.

8. Adolf Erman, *Literature of the Ancient Egyptians* (London: Methuen and Co., Ltd., 1927), p. 109.

9. See André Monglond, *Histoire intérieure du préromantisme français* (Grenoble: Editions B. Arthaud, 1929); Walter Jackson Bate, *From Classic to Romantic* (Cambridge: Harvard University Press, 1949); Ernst Cassirer, *The Philosophy of the Enlightenment,* tr. by Fritz C. A. Koelin and James P. Pettegrove (Princeton: University Press, 1951).

10. Christopher Hussey, *The Picturesque* (London: G. P. Putnam's Sons, 1927); B. Sprague Allen, *Tides in English Taste,* 1619-1800 (2 vols.; Cambridge: Harvard University Press, 1937), vol. 2, pp. 186-99.

11. Monglond, pp. 115, 203ff.

12. *Ibid.*

13. Arthur O. Lovejoy, "The Parallel of Deism and Classicism," *Essays in the History of Ideas* (Baltimore, The Johns Hopkins Press, 1948), reprinted from *Modern Philology,* February, 1932.

14. Locquin, p. 196.

15. See Rogerson.

16. Monglond, p. 187.

17. Leslie, pp. 85, 121.

18. John W. Dodds, *The Age of Paradox* (New York: Rinehart and Co., Inc., 1952), p. 259.

19. Duval, p. 194.

20. *Journal,* May 15, 1855 and February 22, 1860, pp. 462, 669.

21. *Journal,* September 2, 1854 and June 30, 1824, pp. 420-21, 98.

22. Séché, p. 129.

23. Leslie, pp. 24, 273, 281.

24. Charles Baudelaire, Salon of 1846, *The Mirror of Art,* tr. and ed. by Jonathan Mayne (New York: Phaidon Publishers, Inc., 1955), p. 103.

25. *Journal,* April 7, 1849, pp. 194-95.

26. Cited by E. H. Gombrich, "Imagery and Art in the Romantic Period," *The Burlington Magazine,* 91, June 1949, pp. 153-59.

27. Delécluze, *Journal,* pp. 66-67.

28. Heine, pp. 35-36.

29. *Journal,* August 8, 1856, p. 516.

30. *Journal,* May 7, 1824, p. 86 and notes of c. 1840, p. 712.

31. Gombrich, *Art and Illusion,* p. 38, and "The Renaissance Concept of Artistic Progress and Its Consequences."

32. George Boas, "Il Faut être de son temps," *Journal of Aesthetics and Art Criticism,* Spring 1941, pp. 52-65.

33. *Journal,* March 16, 1857, p. 579 and notes of 1847, p. 179.

34. See Gombrich, *Art and Illusion;* Ernst Schachtel, *Metamorphosis* (New York: Basic Books, 1959).

35. Locquin, pp. 236-37.

36. *Journal,* March 7, 1847, p. 156. See also Leo Schrade, *Beethoven in France* (New Haven: Yale University Press, 1942).

37. Cited by Mona Wilson, p. 218.

38. See Walter Friedlander, *David to Delacroix* (Cambridge: Harvard University Press, 1952); Fritz Gysin, *Eugène Delacroix: Studien zu seiner künstlerischen Entwicklung* (Strasbourg: J. H. Ed. Heitz, 1929).

39. *Journal,* January 13, 1857, p. 543.

40. *Journal,* November 13, 1857, p. 609.

41. Georges Matoré, "Les Notions de l'art et d'artiste à l'époque romantique," *Revue des Sciences Humaines,* 1951, pp. 120-36.

42. See Josephine Miles, *Pathetic Fallacy in the Nineteenth Century* (Berkeley: University of California Press, 1942).

43. Gombrich, *Art and Illusion,* pp. 190-92; see also "The Principles of Caricature," by Gombrich and Kris, in *Psychoanalytic Explorations in Art,* pp. 189-204.

44. *Journal,* January 11, 1857, p. 533.

45. George Boas, *French Philosophies of the Romantic Period* (Baltimore: The Johns Hopkins Press, 1925), pp. 296ff.

46. Rosenthal, *Du Romantisme au réalisme,* p. 105.

47. Delécluze, *Journal,* pp. 62ff.

48. *Journal,* January 27, 1847, p. 138.

49. *Corot raconté par lui-même et par ses amis* (Vésenaz-Génève: Pierre Cailler, Editeur, 1946), pp. 84, 96.

50. Salon of 1845 and Exposition Universelle, *The Mirror of Art,* pp. 13ff., 205.

51. *Journal,* February 8, 1860, p. 663.

52. Charles Baudelaire, *L'Art romantique* (Génève: Editions Albert Skira, 1945), p. 40.

53. *Ingres raconté,* pp. 19-20, 23-24, 62.

54. Leslie, pp. 5, 25-86.

55. Matoré, pp. 120-36.

56. A. J. Finberg, *The Life of J. M. W. Turner,* R.A. (revised; Oxford: Clarendon Press, 1961), p. 370.

FIVE

1. Thomas Carlyle, "The State of German Literature," *Works,* vol. I, p. 51.

2. *Journal,* June 17, 1855, pp. 471f.

3. Madame Celnart, *The Gentleman and Lady's Book of Politeness* (tr.; Boston: William D. Ticknor, 1836), pp. 42-43.

4. Herbert Dieckmann, "Diderot's Conception of Genius," *Journal of the History of Ideas*, II, April 1941, pp. 151-82.

5. Monglond, p. 191.

6. Silvestre, vol. II, p. 9.

7. Celnart, pp. 42-43.

8. Gower, p. 84.

9. Margaret Miller, "Géricault's Paintings of the Insane," *Journal of the Warburg and Courtauld Institutes*, IV, 1940-41, pp. 151-63.

10. Celnart, pp. 42-43.

11. Delécluze, *Louis-David*, pp. 122, 131. None of the works of the *primitifs* remains, but Delécluze describes them as being very large outline drawings (in his *Journal*, p. 443).

12. Louis Maigron, *Le Romantisme et la mode* (Paris: Librairie Ancienne, Honoré Champion, 1911); *Le Romantisme et les moeurs* (Paris: Librairie Ancienne, Honoré Champion, 1910).

13. Enid Starkie, *Petrus Borel, the Lycanthrope* (London: Faber and Faber, Ltd., 1954), pp. 50-51, 90-91.

14. Frances Trollope, *Paris and the Parisians in 1835* (New York: Harper and Bros., 1836), p. 124.

15. Lawrence Binyon, *The Followers of William Blake* (London: Halton and Truscott Smith, Ltd., 1925); Thomas Wright, *The Life of William Blake* 2 vols.; Olney, Bucks: T. Wright, 1929), vol. II, p. 90.

16. Maigron, *Le Romantisme et la mode*, pp. 51-93. See also G. M. Young (ed.), *Early Victorian England, 1830-65* (London: Oxford University Press, 1934), p. 427; Ellen Moers, *The Dandy* (New York: Viking, 1960).

17. Maigron, *Le Romantisme et les moeurs*, p. 138.

18. Haydon, vol. I, p. 396.

19. Whitley, 1800-1820, p. 184; Layard, pp. 123, 272.

20. *Journal*, March 24, 1855, pp. 457-58.

21. Finberg, pp. 234ff., 364; Philip Gilbert Hamerton, *The Life of J. M. W. Turner, R. A.* (Boston: Roberts Brothers, 1882), pp. 121, 129, 134; Whitley, 1821-1837, p. 198.

22. Delécluze, *Journal*, pp. 66-67; *Louis-David*, p. 270.

23. Eudo Mason, *The Mind of Henry Fuseli* (London: Routledge and Kegan Paul, 1951).

24. Crabb Robinson, quoted by Symons, p. 237.

25. This has been demonstrated by J. Bronowski, *William Blake* (Hammondsworth, Middlesex: Penguin Books, 1954).

26. Leslie, pp. 12, 73, 270-71; Whitley, 1821-1837, pp. 329ff.

27. Baudelaire, *L'Art romantique*, p. 35.

28. *Journal*, April 15 and May 16, 1823, pp. 46, 48.

29. *Journal*, April 28, 1853, p. 298.

30. *Journal*, October 12, 1859, p. 647; October 16, 1850, pp. 248-49.

31. Baudelaire, *The Mirror of Art*, pp. 125-26.

SIX

1. See J. B. Bury, *The Idea of Progress* (New York: Dover Publications, 1932).

2. Locquin, p. 164.

3. Charles Mitchell, "Benjamin West's 'Death of General Wolfe' and the Popular History Piece," *Journal of the Warburg and Courtauld Institutes,* VII, 1944, pp. 20-33; Edgar Wind, "The Revolution of History Painting," *Journal of the Warburg and Courtauld Institutes,* II, 1938, pp. 116-27.

4. Locquin, p. 280.

5. Edgar Wind, "The Sources of David's 'Horaces'," *Journal of the Warburg and Courtauld Institutes,* IV, 1940-41, pp. 124-38; Delécluze, *Louis-David,* pp. 20ff.

6. Locquin, pp. 165-70, 280.

7. Auguste Viatte, *Les Sources occultes du romantisme,* 1770-1820 (2 vols.; Paris: Librairie Ancienne Honoré Champion, 1928).

8. Delécluze, *Louis-David,* p. 33.

9. *Ibid.,* pp. 158-59.

10. Samuel Rocheblave, *L'Art et le goût en France de 1600 à 1900* (Paris: Librairie Armand Colin, 1923), pp. 210-11.

11. Harold Talbot Parker, *The Cult of Antiquity and the French Revolutionaries* (Chicago: The University of Chicago Press, 1937), pp. 115, 131ff.

12. Delécluze, *Louis-David,* p. 211.

13. Whitley, 1800-1820, p. 271.

14. He did this painting in 1807. See Haydon, vol. I, p. 87; Clarke Olney, *Benjamin Robert Haydon, Historical Painter* (Athens: The University of Georgia Press, 1952), p. 50.

15. Delécluze, *Louis-David,* p. 234 and *Journal,* pp. 65, 329, 345; Rosenthal, *La Peinture romantique,* p. 34; François Benoit, *L'Art français sous la Révolution et l'Empire* (Paris: Société Française d'Editions d'Art, 1897), p. 438.

16. Delécluze, *Journal.*

17. Whitley, 1800-1820, p. 271.

18. *Ibid.* Constable, pp. 71-72.

19. See Wind, "The Sources of David's 'Horaces'."

20. See Alfred Cobban, *In Search of Humanity* (New York: George Braziller, 1960), pp. 194-206.

21. Whitley, 1800-1820, p. 241.

22. Escholier, *Gros.*

23. See Kris, "The Image of the Artist," in *Psychoanalytic Explorations in Art,* pp. 64-84.

24. Delécluze, *Journal,* p. 68. See also Claudius Grillet, *Le Diable dans la littérature au XIXe siècle* (Paris: Emmanuel Vitte, Editeur, 1934).

25. Heine, p. 26.

26. Maigron, *Le Romantisme et les moeurs,* p. 370.

27. René Canat, *L'Héllenisme des romantiques* (Paris: Marcel Didier, 1951), p. 310.

28. Delécluze, *Louis-David,* p. 96.

29. Maigron, *Le Romantisme et les moeurs.*

30. Lady Sydney Morgan, *France in 1829-30* (2 vols.; London: Saunders and Otley, 1831), vol. I, p. 103.

31. Heine, p. 78.

32. *Ibid.,* p. 22.

33. Whitley, 1800-1820, p. 313; 1821-1837, p. 11.

34. Mona Wilson, p. 219.

35. Henderson, p. 84.

36. *Journal,* October 20, 1853, p. 335.

37. Whitley, 1821-1837, p. 142.

38. Heine, p. 26.

39. *Journal,* May 22, 1847, p. 166.

40. T. S. R. Boase, *English Art 1800-70.* (London: Oxford University Press, 1959), p. 170. For various aspects of Romantic imagery, see also The Tate Gallery and the Arts Council Gallery of London, *The Romantic Movement,* Fifth Exhibition to Celebrate the Tenth Anniversary of the Council of Europe, The Arts Council of Great Britain, 1959.

41. See Lorenz Eitner, "The Open Window and the Storm-Tossed Boat," *The Art Bulletin,* 37, December 1955, pp. 281-90; T. S. R. Boase, "Shipwrecks in English Romantic Painting," *Journal of the Warburg and Courtauld Institutes,* 22, 1959, pp. 332-46. For these themes in literature, see W. H. Auden, *The Enchafèd Flood, or The Romantic Iconography of the Sea* (New York: Random House, 1950).

42. *Journal,* November 21, 1857, pp. 610-11.

43. Elie Halévy, *The Triumph of Reform, 1830-1841,* tr. by E. E. Watkins and D. A. Baker (London: Ernest Benn, Ltd., 1949), p. 282.

44. See Mario Praz, *The Hero in Eclipse in Victorian Fiction,* tr. by Angus Davidson (London, New York: Oxford University Press, 1956).

45. Salon of 1859, *The Mirror of Art,* p. 283.

46. Dodds, p. 259.

SEVEN

1. The most famous of these pictures are Hogarth's *Garrick and His Wife* and David's *Lavoisier and His Wife.* See Wind, "The Sources of David's 'Horaces'."

2. Marcel Moraud, *Le Romantisme français en Angleterre de 1814 à 1848* (Paris: Librairie Ancienne Honoré Champion, 1933), pp. 419-20.

3. Locquin, p. 163.

4. Louis Réau, *Fragonard, sa vie et son oeuvre* (Bruxelles: Elsevier, 1956).

5. Waterhouse, "English Painting and France in the Eighteenth Century."

6. Locquin, p. 50.

7. Crane Brinton, *The Anatomy of Revolution* (New York: W. W. Norton and Co., Inc., 1938).

8. Monglond, p. 103.

9. Helen Rosenau, *The Painter Jacques-Louis David* (London: Nicholson and Watson, 1948), p. 56.

10. Charles Blanc, *Histoire des peintres de toutes les écoles* (14 vols.; Paris: Jules Renouard, 1861-70), vol. III; Charles Clément, *Prud'hon, sa vie, ses oeuvres et sa correspondance* (Paris: Didier et Cie., 1880).

11. Locquin, pp. 251, 235.

12. *Ibid.,* p. 251.

13. Boase, "Shipwrecks in English Romantic Painting."

14. See Hussey.

15. Mason, p. 36. See also Ruthven Todd, *Tracks in the Snow* (London: The Grey Walls Press, 1946).

16. Boase, *English Art 1800-70.*

17. Gombrich, "Imagery and Art in the Romantic Period."

18. Delécluze, *Journal,* p. 477. See also Emile Durkheim, *Suicide,* tr. by John A. Spaulding and George Simpson (Glencoe, Illinois: The Free Press, 1951), p. 203.

19. The term dates from around 1840. It was invented to describe the tension between the Moslem world, France, Britain, and Russia, the new bogey in the Near East. See Halévy, *The Triumph of Reform,* p. 268.

20. *Ingres raconté,* p. 111.

21. Benedict Nicolson, "The 'Raft' from the point of view of subject-matter," *The Burlington Magazine,* August 1954, pp. 241-49.

22. Whitley, p. 299.

23. Finberg, p. 379; John Alford, "Romanticism via Ruskin," *Art News,* 42, December 1943, pp. 10-13.

24. Leslie, p. 76.

25. Canat, *L'Héllenisme des romantiques,* p. 302.

26. *Journal,* May 11, 1824, p. 87.

27. Escholier, *Gros,* p. 10.

28. See George Boas, *The Happy Beast in French Thought of the Seventeenth Century* (Baltimore: The Johns Hopkins Press, 1933); Arthur O. Lovejoy and George Boas, *Primitivism and Related Ideas in Antiquity* (Baltimore: The Johns Hopkins Press, 1935); Frances Yates, "Transformations of Dante's Ugolino," *Journal of the Warburg and Courtauld Institutes,* 14, 1951, pp. 92-117.

29. Maigron, *Le Romantisme et la mode,* p. 194.

30. See R. H. Mottram and E. P. Lascelles in G. M. Young, ed., *Early Victorian England,* 1830-65 (2 vols.; London: Oxford University Press, 1934), vol. 1, pp. 155-223, vol. 2, pp. 317-47.

31. Baron Guillibert, *Le Peintre Granet* (Paris: Plon-Nourrit et Cie., 1904), p. 14.

32. See Halévy, *England in 1815,* pp. 566ff.

33. Whitley, 1800-1820, pp. 84-85.

34. Marcel Moraud, *Le Romantisme français en Angleterre de 1814 à 1848* (Paris: Librairie Ancienne Honoré Champion, 1933), pp. 419-20.

35. Whitley, 1821-1837, p. 234.

36. William Gaunt and F. Gordon Roe, *Etty and the Nude* (Essex: F. Lewis, Publishers, Ltd., 1943), pp. 17, 22.

37. Vigée-Lebrun, pp. 177, 185.

38. Crane Brinton, *French Revolutionary Legislation on Illegitimacy,* 1789-1804 (Cambridge: Harvard University Press, 1936); Louis Delzons, *La Famille française et son évolution* (Paris: Librairie Armand Colin, 1913), pp. 17ff.; *Monglond,* p. 192; Delécluze, *Louis-David,* p. 117.

39. *Un Salon de Paris, 1824 à 1864* (Paris: E. Dentu, Editeur, 1866).

40. Maigron, *Le Romantisme et la mode,* pp. 196ff.

41. Locquin, pp. 153-57, 229; Whitley, 1821-1837, p. 212.

42. *Journal,* May 7, 1824, p. 85. For manifestations of sadomasochism in literature, see Mario Praz, *The Romantic Agony* (London, New York: Oxford University Press, 1951).

43. Haydon, vol. I, p. 145; vol. II, p. 504.

44. Séché, p. 165.

45. *Ingres raconté,* p. 11.

46. Tocqueville, p. 118.

47. Gaunt, pp. 17, 22.

48. Thomas Balston, *John Martin, His Life and Works* (London: Gerald Duckworth and Colk Ltd., 1947), p. 107.

49. *Journal,* November 20, 1857, p. 554.

50. Oppé, p. 113.

EIGHT

1. William James, "Great Men, Great Thoughts, and the Environment," *Atlantic Monthly,* 46, October 1880, pp. 441-59.

2. See, for instance, Edward C. Tolman and Egon Brunswik, "The Organism and the Causal Texture of the Environment," *The Psychological Review,* 42, January 1935, pp. 43-77; Gotthard Booth, "The Role of Physical Form in Psychodynamics," *Psychoanalysis and the Psychoanalytic Review,* 47, Spring 1960, pp. 51-62; Gideon Sjoberg, "Contradictory Functional Requirements and Social Systems," *Conflict Resolution,* IV, June 1960, pp. 198-208.

3. For other criticisms of art as communication, see George Boas, "Communication in Dewey's Aesthetics," *Journal of Aesthetics and Art Criticism,* December 1953, pp. 177-83; E. H. Gombrich, "Psychoanalysis and the History of Art," *Freud and the Twentieth Century,* Benjamin Nelson, ed. (New York: Meridian Books, Inc., 1957), and "On Physiognomic Perception," *Daedalus,* Winter 1960, pp. 222-41.

4. *Journal,* February 22, 1860, p. 668.

Index

Some Other Spectrum Books

* Also available in limited clothbound edition.